The PRIMARY SOURCE

Historical Documents:
Pre-Revolutionary America

by

Julia Hargrove

Volume One

ABOUT THE AUTHOR

JULIA HARGROVE was born in San Francisco, California, and grew up in Colorado Springs, Colorado. She received her B.A. degree in History and English from Western State College, Gunnison, Colorado, in 1969, and her M.A. degree in American History from the University of Texas at Austin in 1970. She has been a teacher at Doherty High School in Colorado Springs since 1976 and has used much of the material in this series in her American history classes.

Copyright 1987. Perfection Learning Corporation, Logan, Iowa 51546

TABLE OF CONTENTS

INTRODUCTION

Effective history teaching goes beyond the information presented in a textbook. To bring history alive for students, the teacher needs to enrich the history curriculum with materials that will hold the students' interest while at the same time giving them a different perspective on their historical studies.

The Primary Source is designed to help fill this need. In this series students go beyond the textbook to read original documents from American history. In the process, they learn firsthand about the people and events described in their textbooks. At the same time, they get experience with one of the historian's key tasks: analyzing and interpreting primary source material.

Each volume of *The Primary Source* presents a different series of historical documents. Each document is accompanied by a study guide containing two sets of questions. The first set, **Facts and Concepts**, asks students to critically examine and analyze the important ideas in the document. The second set, **For Further Understanding**, takes the students outside the document to solve historical and practical problems.

Each volume is fully reproducible, enabling the teacher to give each student his or her own copy of a document and its study guide. An answer key for the teacher is included at the end of each volume.

In Volume 1 students are introduced to historical documents of the pre-revolutionary period. These documents show the background of American political and constitutional development, and highlight some of the very real problems the early Americans faced in settling a new world.

MAGNA CARTA

1215

The Magna Carta is one of the most important documents in world history. Although it was designed to protect the interests of medieval English nobles, not common people, it was a novel attempt at designing a constitutional government. The ideas of the Magna Carta were later used by framers of democratic governments, including the authors of the Declaration of Independence and the Constitution.

John, by the grace of God, king of England, lord of Ireland, duke of Normandy and Aquitaine, and count of Anjou, to the archbishops, bishops, abbots, earls, barons, justiciars, foresters, sheriffs, stewards, servants, and to all his bailiffs and faithful subjects, greeting. Knowing that we, out of reverence for God and for the salvation of our soul and those of all our ancestors and heirs, for the honour of God and the exaltation of holy church, and for the reform of our realm, on the advice of our venerable fathers, Stephen, archbishop of Canterbury, primate of all England and cardinal of the holy Roman church, . . . and others, our faithful subjects:

[1] In the first place have granted to God, and by this our present charter confirmed for us and our heirs for ever that the English church shall be free, and shall have its rights, undiminished and its liberties unimpaired; and it is our will that it be thus observed; which is evident from the fact that, before the quarrel between us and our barons began, we willingly and spontaneously granted and by our charter confirmed the freedom of elections which is reckoned most important and very essential to the English church, and obtained confirmation of it from the lord pope Innocent III; the which we will observe and we wish our heirs to observe it in good faith for ever. We have also granted to all free men of our kingdom, for ourselves and our heirs for ever, all the liberties written below, to be had and held by them and their heirs of us and our heirs.

[2] If any of our earls or barons or others holding of us in chief by knight service dies, and at his death his heir be of full age and owe relief he shall have his inheritance on payment of the old relief, . . .

[3] If, however, the heir of any such be under age and a ward, he shall have his inheritance when he comes of age without paying relief and without making fine.

[4] The guardian of the land of such an heir who is under age shall take from the land of the heir no more than reasonable revenues, reasonable customary dues and reasonable services and that without destruction and waste of men or goods; . . .

[5] Moreover, so long as he has the wardship of the land, the guardian shall keep in repair the houses, parks, preserves, ponds, mills and other things pertaining to the land out of the revenues from it; and he shall restore to the heir when he comes of age his land fully stocked with ploughs and the means of husbandry according to what the season of husbandry requires and the revenues of the land can reasonably bear.

[6] Heirs shall be married without disparagement, yet so that before the marriage is contracted those nearest in blood to the heir shall have notice.

[7] A widow shall have her marriage portion and inheritance forthwith and without difficulty after the death of her husband;

nor shall she pay anything to have her dower or her marriage portion or the inheritance which she and her husband held on the day of her husband's death and she may remain in her husband's house for forty days after his death, within which time her dower shall be assigned to her.

[8] No widow shall be forced to marry so long as she wishes to live without a husband, provided that she gives security not to marry without our consent if she holds of us, or without the consent of her lord of whom she holds, if she holds of another.

[9] Neither we nor our bailiffs will seize for any debt any land or rent, so long as the chattels of the debtor are sufficient to repay the debt; nor will those who have gone surety for the debtor be distrained so long as the principal debtor is himself able to pay the debt; . . .

[10] If anyone who has borrowed from the Jews any sum, great or small, dies before it is repaid, the debt shall not bear interest as long as the heir is under age, of whomsoever he holds; . . .

[12] No scutage or aid shall be imposed in our kingdom unless by common counsel of our kingdom, except for ransoming our person, for making our eldest son a knight, and for once marrying our oldest daughter; and for these only a reasonable aid shall be levied . . .

[14] And to obtain the common counsel of the kingdom about the assessing of an aid (except in the three cases aforesaid) or of a scutage, we will cause to be summoned the archbishops, bishops, abbots, earls and greater barons, individually by our letters . . . for a fixed date, namely, after the expiry of at least forty days, and to a fixed place; and in all letters of such summons we will specify the reason for the summons. And

when the summons has thus been made, the business shall proceed on the day appointed, according to the counsel of those present, though not all have come who were summoned.

[15] We will not in future grant any one the right to take an aid from his free men, except for ransoming his person, for making his eldest son a knight and for once marrying his eldest daughter, and for these only a reasonable aid shall be levied . . .

[20] A free man shall not be amerced for a trivial offence except in accordance with the degree of the offence, and for a grave offence he shall be amerced in accordance with its gravity, yet saving his way of living; and a merchant in the same way, saving his stock-in-trade; and a villein shall be amerced in the same way, saving his means of livelihood—if they have fallen into our mercy: and none of the aforesaid amercements shall be imposed except by the oath of good men of the neighbourhood . . .

[26] If anyone holding a lay fief of us dies and our sheriff or bailiff shows our letters patent of summons for a debt that the deceased owed us, it shall be lawful for our sheriff or bailiff to attach and make a list of chattels of the deceased found upon the lay fief to the value of that debt under the supervision of law-worthy men, provided that none of the chattels shall be removed until the debt which is manifest has been paid to us in full; . . .

[27] If any free man dies without leaving a will, his chattels shall be distributed by his nearest kinsfolk and friends under the supervision of the church, saving to every one the debts which the deceased owed him.

[28] No constable or other

bailiff of ours shall take anyone's corn or other chattels unless he pays on the spot in cash for them or can delay payment by arrangement with the seller . . .

[30] No sheriff, or bailiff of ours, or anyone else shall take the horses or carts of any free man for transport work save with the agreement of that freeman.

[31] Neither we nor our bailiffs will take, for castles or other works of ours, timber which is not ours, except with the agreement of him whose timber it is.

[32] We will not hold for more than a year and a day the lands of those convicted of felony, and then the lands shall be handed over to the lords of the fiefs . . .

[36] Nothing shall be given or taken in future for the writ of inquisition of life or limbs: instead it shall be granted free of charge and not refused . . .

[38] No bailiff shall in future put anyone to trial upon his own bare word, without reliable witnesses produced for this purpose.

[39] No free man shall be arrested or imprisoned or disseised or outlawed or exiled or in any way victimised, neither will we attack him or send anyone to attack him, except by the lawful judgment of his peers or by the law of the land.

[40] To no one will we sell, to no one will we refuse or delay right or justice.

[41] All merchants shall be able to go out of and come into England safely and securely and stay and travel throughout England, as well by land as by water, for buying and selling by the ancient and right customs free from all evil tolls, except in time of war and if they are of the land that is at war with us . . .

[45] We will not make justices, constables, sheriffs or bailiffs save of such as know the law of the kingdom and mean to observe it well.

[46] All barons who have founded abbeys for which they have charters of the kings of England or ancient tenure shall have the custody of them during vacancies, as they ought to have . . .

[48] All evil customs connected with forests and warrens, foresters and warreners, sheriffs and their officials, riverbanks and their wardens shall immediately be inquired into in each county by twelve sworn knights of the same county who are to be chosen by good men of the same county, and within forty days of the completion of the inquiry shall be utterly abolished by them so as never to be restored, provided that we, or our justiciar if we are not in England, know of it first.

[49] We will immediately return all hostages and charters given to us by Englishmen, as security for peace or faithful service . . .

[52] If anyone has been disseised of or kept out of his lands, castles, franchises or his right by us without the legal judgment of his peers, we will immediately restore them to him: and if a dispute arises over this, then let it be decided by the judgment of the twenty-five barons who are mentioned below in the clause for securing the peace . . .

[55] All fines made with us unjustly and against the law of the land, and all amercements imposed unjustly and against the law of the land, shall be entirely remitted, or else let them be settled by the judgment of the twenty-five barons who are mentioned below in the clause for securing the peace, or by the

judgment of the majority of the same, along with the aforesaid Stephen, archbishop of Canterbury, if he can be present, ...

[57] If we have disseised or kept out Welshmen from lands or liberties or other things without the legal judgment of their peers in England or in Wales, they shall be immediately restored to them; and if a dispute arises over this, then let it be decided in the March by the judgment of their peers ...

[60] All these aforesaid customs and liberties which we have granted to be observed in our kingdom as far as it pertains to us towards our men, all of our kingdom, clerks as well as laymen, shall observe as far as it pertains to them towards their men.

[61] Since, moreover, for God and the betterment of our kingdom and for the better allaying of the discord that has arisen between us and our barons we have granted all these things aforesaid, wishing them to enjoy the use of them unimpaired and unshaken for ever, we give and grant them the under-written security, namely, that the barons shall choose any twenty-five barons of the kingdom they wish, who must with all their might observe, hold and cause to be observed, the peace and liberties which we have granted and confirmed to them by this present charter of ours, so that if we, or our justiciar, or our bailiffs or any one of our servants offend in any way against anyone or transgress any of the articles of the peace or the security and the offence be notified to four of the aforesaid twenty-five barons, those four barons shall come to us, or to our justiciar if we are out of the kingdom, and, laying the transgression before us, shall petition us to have that transgression corrected without delay. And if we do not correct the transgression, or if we are out of the kingdom, if our justiciar does not correct it, within forty days, reckoning from the time it was brought to our notice or to that of our justiciar if we were out of the kingdom, the aforesaid four barons shall refer that case to the rest of the twenty-five barons and those twenty-five barons together with the community of the whole land shall distrain and distress us in every way they can, namely, by seizing castles, lands, possessions, and in such other ways as they can, saving our person and the persons of our queen and our children, until, in their opinion, amends have been made; and when amends have been made, they shall obey us as they did before. And let anyone in the land who wishes take an oath to obey the orders of the said twenty-five barons for the execution of all the aforesaid matters, and with them to distress us as much as he can, and we publicly and freely give anyone leave to take the oath who wishes to take it and we will never prohibit anyone from taking it. Indeed, all those in the land who are unwilling of themselves and of their own accord to take an oath to the twenty-five barons to help them to distrain and distress us, we will make them take the oath as aforesaid at our command. And if any of the twenty-five barons dies or leaves the country or is in any other way prevented from carrying out the things aforesaid, the rest of the aforesaid twenty-five barons shall choose as they think fit another one in his place, and he shall take the oath like the rest. In all matters the execution of which is committed to these twenty-five barons, if it should happen that these twenty-five are

present yet disagree among themselves about anything, or if some of those summoned will not or cannot be present, that shall be held as fixed and established which the majority of those present ordained or commanded, exactly as if all the twenty-five had consented to it; and the said twenty-five shall swear that they will faithfully observe all the things aforesaid and will do all they can to get them observed. And we will procure nothing from anyone, either personally or through anyone else, whereby any of these concessions and liberties might be revoked or diminished; and if any such thing is procured, let it be void and null, and we will never use it either personally or through another.

[62] And we have fully remitted and pardoned to everyone all the ill-will, indignation and rancour that have arisen between us and our men, clergy and laity, from the time of the quarrel . . .

[63] Wherefore we wish and firmly enjoin that the English church shall be free, and that the men in our kingdom shall have and hold all the aforesaid liberties, rights and concessions well and peacefully, freely and quietly, fully and completely, for themselves and their heirs from us and our heirs, in all matters and in all places for ever, as is aforesaid. An oath, moreover, has been taken, as well on our part as on the part of the barons, that all these things aforesaid shall be observed in good faith and without evil disposition. Witness the above-mentioned and many others. Given by our hand in the meadow which is called Runnymede between Windsor and Staines on the fifteenth day of June, in the seventeenth year of our reign.

MAGNA CARTA

1215

I. **Facts and Concepts**

1. Who was the king of England at the time this document was signed?

   _____

2. Where and when was this document signed?

   _____

3. Sections 2 through 8 concern inheritance laws and the rights of survivors of deceased people. Answer the following questions based on those sections.

   a. Look up the word "relief" in a dictionary or history book and write down its meaning as it was used in feudal England.

   _____

   _____

   b. Look up "ward" and write down its meaning. What problem about wards does Section 4 try to solve?

   _____

   _____

   c. Sections 7 and 8 concern widows. What could a person gain by forcing a widow to marry him?

   _____

   _____

4. A farmer has a small plot of land, a house, and about three pounds worth of chattels (moveable property). He borrows one pound to buy seed. According to Section 9, what part of his property will be taken from him if he cannot repay the loan?

   _____

   _____

5. Find a section in the document that benefits merchants. What right are merchants guaranteed in this section? Quote the section to support your answer.

_____

_____

6. Section 12 says that, with certain exceptions, the king cannot lay taxes "unless by common counsel." What is important about this statement?

_____

_____

7. Section 20 concerns punishments for offenses. Read this section and answer the following questions.

   a. Look up the word "amerce" and write down its meaning as it is used in this document.

   _____

   b. What important limit is placed on amercements by this section?

   _____

   _____

8. What does Section 38 prohibit?

   _____

   _____

9. Read Section 52 and answer the following questions.

   a. Look up the word "disseise" (also spelled "disseize") and write down its meaning.

   _____

   b. Under what circumstances could an owner have disseised lands returned to him?

   _____

   _____

10. What does Section 39 prohibit?

_____

_____

11. What is Section 45 designed to prevent?

_____

_____

12. Section 61 discusses the council of twenty-five barons. Read the description of this council and answer the following questions.

a. What is the purpose of the council?

_____

_____

b. Briefly describe the process outlined for reporting and correcting abuses.

_____

_____

13. What action does Section 63 include to insure that the provisions of the document would be carried out?

_____

_____

II. For Further Understanding

14. The words "we" and "our" are used often in this document? Who do they refer to?

_____

15. Explain briefly the situation between King John and the barons of England at the time the Magna Carta was written.

_____

_____

_____

_____

16. The English are said to have an "unwritten constitution." What does this mean? What is their "unwritten constitution" based on?

_____

_____

_____

17. According to Section 12, "common counsel" is needed for the king to lay taxes. What slogan from the revolutionary era in America summarizes the ideas in this paragraph?

_____

18. Read Section 39. What amendment to the U.S. Constitution guarantees the same rights described in this section?

_____

MAYFLOWER COMPACT

1620

Upon reaching their new home in America, the Pilgrims formed an agreement, vowing that each member of the community would submit to the laws and institutions that the community established. This agreement is known as the Mayflower Compact, named for the ship that brought the Pilgrims to America. The Mayflower Compact was the first document guaranteeing self-government ever signed in America, and its principles are very important to American political development.

IN The Name of God, Amen. We, whose names are underwritten, the loyal Subjects of our dread Sovereign Lord King *James*, by the Grace of God, of Great Britain, France, and Ireland, King, Defender of the Faith, &c. Having undertaken for the Glory of God, and Advancement of the Christian Faith, and the Honour of our King and Country, a Voyage to plant the first colony in the northern Parts of Virginia; Do by these Presents, solemnly and mutually in the Presence of God and one another, covenant and combine ourselves together into a civil Body Politick, for our better Ordering and Preservation, and Furtherance of the Ends aforesaid; And by Virtue hereof do enact, constitute, and frame, such just and equal Laws, Ordinances, Acts, Constitutions, and Offices, from time to time, as shall be thought most meet and convenient for the general Good of the Colony; unto which we promise all due Submission and Obedience. In WITNESS whereof we have hereunto subscribed our names at Cape Cod the eleventh of November, in the Reign of our Sovereign Lord King James of England, France, and Ireland, the eighteenth and of Scotland, the fifty-fourth. *Anno Domini,* 1620

MAYFLOWER COMPACT

1620

Facts and Concepts

1. Look up the following words or phrases in a dictionary or history book and write down their definitions as they are used in this document: body politic, covenant, civil, ordinances.

_____

_____

_____

_____

_____

2. In what day, month, and year was this compact written?

_____

3. Who was king of Great Britain at the time this compact was written?

_____

4. According to the document, where had the Pilgrims planned to land in the New World? What is the present name of the area where they actually landed?

_____

_____

5. Quote a phrase from the document that shows the Pilgrims had a strong religious faith.

_____

_____

6. Quote a phrase from the document that shows the Pilgrims intended to make their own laws.

_____

_____

_____

II. For Further Understanding

7. Why did Pilgrim leaders believe it was necessary to have the Mayflower Compact?

_____

_____

_____

8. Why did the Pilgrims travel to the New World?

_____

_____

_____

9. Who issued the Pilgrims a land grant to settle in America? Why did they not settle on this land grant?

_____

_____

_____

10. Did the Mayflower Compact require the Pilgrims to establish a democratic government? Explain your answer.

_____

_____

_____

PETITION OF RIGHT

1628

The Petition of Right was drawn up by the English Parliament in 1628 to put a stop to royal actions that Parliament considered illegal. It is important because it declared the actions of Parliament to be more important than the wishes of the king. Many of the ideas contained in the Petition of Right were later included in the Declaration of Independence and the Constitution.

The Petition exhibited to his Majesty by the Lords Spiritual and Temporal and Commons in this present Parliament assembled concerning divers rights and liberties of the subject.

To the King's Most Excellent Majesty

Humbly show unto our Sovereign Lord the King the Lords Spiritual and Temporal and Commons in Parliament assembled, that whereas it is declared and enacted by a statute made in the time of the reign of King Edward the First commonly called Statutum de Tallagio non Concedendo, that no tallage or aid should be laid or levied by the King or his heirs in this realm without the good will and assent of the archbishops, bishops, earls, barons, knights, burgesses and other the freemen of the commonalty of this realm; and by authority of Parliament holden in the five and twentieth year of the reign of King Edward the Third it is declared and enacted, that from henceforth no person should be compelled to make any loans to the King against his will because such loans were against reason and the franchise of the land, and by other laws of this realm it is provided that none should be charged by any charge or imposi-

tion called a benevolence nor by such like charge, by which the statutes before mentioned and other the good laws and statutes of this realm your subjects have inherited this freedom, that they should not be compelled to contribute to any tax, tallage, aid or other like charge not set by common consent in Parliament.

II. Yet, nevertheless of late divers commissions directed to sundry commissioners in several counties with instructions have issued, by means whereof your people have been in divers places assembled and required to lend certain sums of money unto your Majesty, and many of them upon their refusal so to do have had an oath administered unto them not warrantable by the laws or statutes of this realm, and have been constrained to become bound to make appearance and give attendance before your Privy Council and in other places; and others of them have been therefore imprisoned, confined, and sundry other ways molested and disquieted, and divers other charges have been laid and levied upon your people in several counties by Lord Lieutenants, Deputy Lieutenants, Commissioners for Musters, Justices of Peace and others by command or direction from your Majesty or your Privy Council against the laws and free customs of the realm.

III. And where also by the statute called the Great Charter of the Liberties of England it is declared and enacted, that no freemen may be taken or imprisoned or be disseised of his freehold or liberties or his free customs or be outlawed or exiled or in any manner destroyed, but by the lawful judgement of his peers or by the law of the land.

IV. And in the eight and

twentieth year of the reign of King Edward the Third it was declared and enacted by authority of Parliament, that no man, of what estate or condition that he be, should be put out of his land or tenement, not taken, nor imprisoned, nor disherited, nor put to death without being brought to answer by due process of law.

V. Nevertheless against the tenor of the said statutes and other the good laws and statutes of your realm to that end provided, divers of your subjects have of late been imprisoned without any cause shown; and when for their deliverance they were brought before your justices by your Majesty's writ of habeas corpus there to undergo and receive as the Court should order, and their Keepers commanded to certify the causes of their detainer, no cause was certified, but that they were detained by your Majesty's special command signified by the Lords of your Privy Council, and yet were returned back to several prisons without being charged with any thing to which they might make answer according to the law.

VI. And whereas of late great companies of soldiers and mariners have been dispersed into divers counties of the realm, and the inhabitants against their will have been compelled to receive them into their houses, and there to suffer them to sojourn against the laws and customs of this realm and to the great grievance and vexation of the people.

VII. And whereas also by authority of Parliament in the five and twentieth year of the reign of King Edward the Third it is declared and enacted that no man should be forejudged of life and limb against the form of the Great Charter and the law of the land;

and by the said Great Charter, and other the laws and statutes of this your realm, no man ought to be adjudged to death but by the laws established in this your realm, either by the customs of the same realm or by Act of Parliament, and whereas no offender of what kind soever is exempted from the proceedings to be used and punishments to be inflicted by the laws and statutes of this your realm; nevertheless of late time divers commissions under your Majesty's great seal have issued forth, by which certain persons have been assigned and appointed commissioners with power and authority to proceed within the land according to the justice of martial law against such soldiers or mariners or other dissolute persons joining with them as should commit any murder, robbery, felony, mutiny or other outrage or misdemeanour whatsoever, and by such summary course and order as is agreeable to martial law and as is used in armies in time of war to proceed to the trial and condemnation of such offenders, and them to cause to be executed and put to death according to the law martial.

By pretext whereof some of your Majesty's subjects have been by some of the said commissioners put to death, when and where, if by the laws and statutes of the land they had deserved death, by the same laws and statutes also they might and by no other ought to have been judged and executed.

And also sundry grievous offenders by colour thereof claiming an exemption have escaped the punishments due to them by the laws and statutes of this your realm, by reason that divers of your officers and ministers of justice have unjustly refused or forborne to proceed against such offenders according to the same laws and statutes upon pretence that the said offenders were punishable only by martial law and by authority of such commissions as aforesaid. Which commissions and all others of like nature are wholly and directly contrary to the said laws and statutes of this your realm.

VIII. They do therefore humbly pray your most excellent Majesty that no man hereafter be compelled to make or yield any gift, loan, benevolence, tax or such like charge without common consent by Act of Parliament, and that none be called to make answer or take such oath or to give attendance or be confined or otherwise molested or disquieted concerning the same or for refusal thereof. And that no freeman in any such manner as is before mentioned be imprisoned or detained. And that your Majesty would be pleased to remove the said soldiers and mariners, and that your people may not be so burdened in time to come. And that the aforesaid commissions for proceeding by martial law may be revoked and annulled. And that hereafter no commissions of like nature may issue forth to any person or persons whatsoever to be executed as aforesaid, lest by colour of them any of your Majesty's subjects be destroyed or put to death contrary to the laws and franchises of the land.

All which they most humbly pray of your most excellent Majesty as their rights and liberties according to the laws and statutes of this realm, and that your Majesty would also vouchsafe to declare that the awards, doings, and proceedings to the prejudice of your people in any of the premises shall not be drawn hereafter into consequence or example. And that your Majesty would be also graciously pleased for the further comfort and safety of your people to declare your royal will and pleasure, that in the thing aforesaid all your officers and ministers shall serve you according to the laws and statutes of this realm as they tender the honour of your Majesty and the prosperity of this kingdom.

PETITION OF RIGHT

1628

I. Facts and Concepts

1. Who are the "Lords Spiritual and Temporal and Commons"?

_____

2. Read the paragraph beginning "Humbly show unto our ..." and answer the following questions.

   a. Look up the words "tallage" and "benevolence" and write down their definitions as they are used in this document.

   _____

   _____

   _____

   b. What was the king trying to do through all of the actions described in this paragraph?

   _____

   c. In one sentence of your own words, explain the main idea of this paragraph.

   _____

   _____

3. In your own words, explain the main idea of Section III.

   _____

   _____

4. After reading Section IV, look up "due process of law" and write down its definition.

   _____

   _____

5. What is the king accused of in Section V?

   _____

   _____

6. Explain in your own words the grievance described in Section VI.

_____

_____

7. Read Section VII and answer the following questions.

   a. Look up "martial law" and write down its definition.

   _____

   _____

   b. For what purpose had the king used martial law?

   _____

   _____

8. In your own words, describe the main idea of the second paragraph of Section VII.

   _____

   _____

   _____

9. What is the purpose of Section VIII?

   _____

   _____

10. Read the last paragraph of the document and answer the following questions.

    a. Are the writers of the petition asking for new rights, or rights they have already been granted?

    _____

    _____

    b. What do the petitioners ask that the king do in the last sentence of the document?

    _____

    _____

II. For Further Understanding

11. Who was the king of England at the time this petition was presented?

    _____

12. What happened to the king in 1649?

    _____

13. What is another name for the "Great Charter of the Liberties of England" mentioned in Section III?

    _____

14. Which of the amendments in the Bill of Rights of the U.S. Constitution guarantees the same rights as those described in Section III? Quote part of the amendment to support your answer.

    _____

    _____

    _____

    _____

    _____

15. Sections I and II concern the king's methods of taxation. In what way do citizens of the United States have control over the taxes they pay?

    _____

    _____

    _____

    _____

FUNDAMENTAL ORDERS OF CONNECTICUT

1639

In 1639 the leaders of three settlements in Connecticut decided to unite under a written constitution. The document they created, called the Fundamental Orders, set a precedent for constitutional government in America.

Forasmuch as it hath pleased the Allmighty God by the wise disposition of his divyne pruvidence so to Order and dispose of things that we the Inhabitants and Residents of Windsor, Harteford and Wethersfield are now cohabiting and dwelling in and uppon the River of Conectecotte and the Lands thereunto adioyneing; And well knowing where a people are gathered togather the word of God requires that to mayntayne the peace and union of such a people there should be an orderly and decent Government established according to God, to order and dispose of the affayres of the people at all seasons as occasion shall require; doe therefore assotiate and conioyne our selves to be as one Publike State or Commonwelth; and doe, for our selves and our Successors and such as shall be adioyned to us att any tyme hereafter, enter into Combination and Confederation togather, to mayntayne and presearve the liberty and purity of the gospell of our Lord Jesus which we now professe, as also the disciplyne of the Churches, which according to the truth of the said gospell is now practised amongst us; As also in our Civell Affaires to be guided and governed according to such Lawes, Rules, Orders and decrees as shall be made, ordered & decreed, as followeth:—

1. It is Ordered . . . that there shall be yerely two generall Assemblies or Courts, the one the second thursday in Aprill, the other the second thursday in September, following; the first shall be called the Courte of Election, wherein shall be yerely Chosen . . . soe many Magestrats and other publike Officers as shall be found requisitte: Whereof one to be chosen Governour for the yeare ensueing and untill another be chosen, and noe other Magestrate to be chosen for more than one yeare; provided allwayes there be six chosen besids the Governour; which being chosen and sworne according to an Oath recorded for that purpose shall have power to administer justice according to the Lawes here established, and for want thereof according to the rule of the word of God; which choise shall be made by all that are admitted freemen and have taken the Oath of Fidellity, and doe cohabitte within this Jurisdiction, (having beene admitted Inhabitants by the major part of the Towne wherein they live,) or the major parte of such as shall be then present . . .

4. It is Ordered . . . that noe person be chosen Governor above once in two yeares, and that the Governor be alwayes a member of some approved congregation, and formerly of the Magestracy within this Jurisdiction; and all the Magestrats Freemen of this Commonwelth: . . .

5. It is Ordered . . . that to the aforesaid Courte of Election the severall Townes shall send their deputyes, and when the Elections are ended they may proceed in any publike searvice as at other Courts. Also the other Generall Courte in September shall be for makeing of lawes, and any other publike occation, which conserns the good of the Commonwelth . . .

7. It is Ordered . . . that after there are warrants given out for

any of the said Generall Courts, the Constable . . . of ech Towne shall forthwith give notice distinctly to the inhabitants of the same, . . . that at a place and tyme by him or them lymited and sett, they meet and assemble them selves togather to elect and chuse certen deputyes to be att the Generall Courte then following to agitate the afayres of the commonwelth; which said Deputyes shall be chosen by all that are admitted Inhabitants in the severall Townes and have taken the oath of fidellity; provided that non be chosen a Deputy for any Generall Courte which is not a Freeman of this Commonwelth . . .

8. It is Ordered . . . that Wyndsor, Hartford and Wethersfield shall have power, ech Towne, to send fower of their freemen as their deputyes to every Generall Courte; and whatsoever other Townes shall be hereafter added to this Jurisdiction, they shall send so many deputyes as the Courte shall judge meete, a resonable proportion to the number of Freemen that are in the said Townes being to be attended therein; which deputyes shall have the power of the whole Towne to give their voats and alowance to all such lawes and orders as may be for the publike good, and unto which the said Townes are to be bownd.

9. It is ordered . . . that the deputyes thus chosen shall have power and liberty to appoynt a tyme and a place of meeting togather before any Generall Courte to advise and consult of all such things as may concerne the good of the publike, as also to examine their owne Elections . . .

10. It is Ordered . . . that every Generall Courte . . . shall consist of the Governor, or some one chosen to moderate the Court, and 4 other Magestrats at lest, with the major parte of the deputyes of the severall Townes legally chosen;

and in case the Freemen or major parte of them, through neglect or refusall of the Governor and major parte of the magestrats, shall call a Courte, it shall consist of the major parte of Freemen that are present or their deputyes, with a Moderator chosen by them: In which said Generall Courts shall consist the supreme power of the Commonwelth, and they only shall have power to make lawes or repeale them, to graunt levyes, to admitt of Freemen, dispose of lands undisposed of, to severall Townes or persons, and also shall have power to call ether Courte or Magestrate or any other person whatsoever into question for any misdemeanour, and may for just causes displace or deale otherwise according to the nature of the offence; and also may deale in any other matter that concerns the good of this commonwelth, excepte election of Magestrats, which shall be done by the whole boddy of Freemen.

In which Courte the Governour or Moderator shall have power to order the Courte to give liberty of spech, and silence unceasonable and disorderly speakeings, to put all things to voate, and in case the vote be equall to have the casting voice. But non of these Courts shall be adjorned or dissolved without the consent of the major parte of the Court.

11. It is ordered . . . that when any Generall Courte uppon the occations of the Commonwelth have agreed uppon any summe or sommes of mony to be levyed uppon the severall Townes within this Jurisdiction, that a Committee be chosen to sett out and appoynt what shall be the proportion of every Towne to pay of the said levy, provided the Committees be made up of an equall number out of each Towne.

FUNDAMENTAL ORDERS OF CONNECTICUT

1639

Facts and Concepts

1. What three settlements had been founded in Connecticut at the time this document was written?

_____

_____

2. Quote the phrase from the first paragraph of this document by which the people of these three settlements agree to unite under a single government.

_____

_____

3. Read Section 1 and answer the following questions.

a. What is the purpose of the Court of Election?

_____

b. Look up the word "magistrate" (spelled "magestrat" in this document) in a dictionary or history book and write down its definition.

_____

c. Including the governor, how many magistrates are to be elected?

_____

d. What three qualifications must a person meet in order to participate in the election of magistrates?

_____

_____

_____

4. According to Section 5, what is the purpose of the General Court?

_____

_____

5. According to Section 7, what qualification do candidates for the office of deputy have to meet?

_____

6. Quote the phrase in Section 8 showing that new settlements in Connecticut will be allowed to send deputies to the General Court.

_____

_____

_____

7. In your own words, explain the power granted to the deputies in Section 9.

_____

_____

8. Read Section 10 and answer the following questions.

a. What group of people can call a General Court if the governor and the magistrates neglect or refuse to do so?

_____

b. Who or what body is granted supreme power in Connecticut?

_____

c. List in your own words the seven powers granted to the General Courts in this section.

_____

_____

_____

_____

_____

9. List in your own words the four powers given to the governor or moderator of the General Court in the paragraph beginning "In which Courte . . ." in Section 10.

_____

_____

_____

_____

10. Read Section 11 and answer the following questions.

a. What are "sommes of mony to be levyed uppon the severall Townes . . . ?"

_____

b. What is the purpose of the special committee described in this section?

_____

For Further Understanding

11. What leader founded Hartford, Connecticut?

_____

12. Why did settlers leave the Massachusetts Bay colony to found Connecticut?

_____

_____

_____

13. How long was the period of time between the founding of Hartford and the writing of the Fundamental Orders?

_____

MASSACHUSETTS SCHOOL LAWS

1642 and 1647

Massachusetts took the lead in establishing rules for public education. The school laws of 1642 and 1647 provided a model for educational policies in the other colonies.

Massachusetts School Law of 1642

This Cort, taking into consideration the great neglect of many parents & masters in training up their children in learning & labor, & other implyments which may be proffitable to the common wealth, do hereupon order and decree, that in euery towne ye chosen men appointed for managing the prudentiall affajres of the same shall henceforth stand charged with the care of the redresse of this evill, so as they shalbee sufficiently punished by fines for the neglect thereof, upon presentment of the grand jury, or other information or complaint in any Court within this jurisdiction; and for this end they, or the greater number of them, shall have power to take account from time to time of all parents and masters, and of their children, concerning their calling and implyment of their children, especially of their ability to read & understand the principles of religion & the capitall lawes of this country, and to impose fines upon such as shall refuse to render such accounts to them when they shall be required; and they shall have power, with consent of any Court or the magistrate, to put forth apprentices the children of such as they shall (find) not to be able & fitt to employ and bring them up.

They shall take . . . that boyes and girles be not suffered to converse together, so as may occasion any wanton, dishonest, or immodest behavior; & for their better performance of this trust committed to them, they may divide the towne amongst them, appointing to every of the said townesmen a certaine number of families to have special oversight of. They are also to provide that a sufficient quantity of materialls, as hemp, flaxe, ecra, may be raised in their severall townes, & tooles & implements provided for working out the same; & for their assistance in this so needfull and beneficiall imploymt, if they meete wth any difficulty or opposition wch they cannot well master by their own power, they may have recorse to some of the matrats, who shall take such course for their help & incuragmt as the occasion shall require according to justice; & the said townesmen, at the next Cort in those limits, after the end of their year, shall give a briefe account in writing of their proceedings herein, provided that they have bene so required by some Cort or magistrate a month at least before; & this order to continew for two yeares, & till the Cort shall take further order.

Massachusetts School Law of 1647

It being one chiefe project of ye ould deluder, Satan, to keepe men from the knowledge of ye Scriptures, as in former times by keeping ym in an unknowne tongue, so in these latter times by perswading from ye use of tongues, yt so at least ye true sence & meaning of ye originall might be clouded by false glosses of saint seeming deceivers, yet learning may not be buried in ye grave of or fathers in ye church and commonwealth, the Lord assisting or endeavors,—

It is therefore ordered, yet every towneship in this jurisdiction, after ye Lord hath increased your number to 50 housholdrs, shall then forthwith appoint one with in their towne to teach all such children as shall resort to him to write & reade, whose wages shall be paid either by ye parents or masters of such children, or by ye inhabitants in generall, by way of supply, as ye major part of those yet orderly prudentials ye twone shall appoint; provided, those yet send their children be not oppressed by paying much more ym they can have ym taught for in other townes; & it is further ordered, yet where any towne shall increase to ye number of 100 families or househoulders, they shall set up a grammer schoole, ye mr thereof being able to instruct youth so farr as they shall be fitted for ye university, provided, yet if any towne neglect ye performance hereof above one yeare, yet every such towne shall pay 5 pounds to ye next schoole till they shall performe this order.

MASSACHUSETTS SCHOOL LAWS

1642 and 1647

I. Facts and Concepts

A. Massachusetts School Law of 1642

1. What problem is stated as the reason for this law?

_____

_____

2. What people are made responsible for education in their towns?

_____

3. What punishment was prescribed if these people did not carry out their duties regarding education?

_____

4. How were those responsible for education allowed to find out whether or not children were being educated?

_____

_____

5. Quote the reason given in the document for not allowing boys and girls to converse together.

_____

_____

6. What two types of training does this document require?

_____

_____

B. Massachusetts School Law of 1647

7. In your own words, state the reason given in the first paragraph for requiring children to learn to read and write.

_____

_____

8. What does this document require townships of more than fifty households to do about education?

_____

_____

9. What is required of townships of more than one hundred households?

_____

_____

10. What was the goal of the schools set up in townships of more than one hundred households?

_____

_____

For Further Understanding

11. What is the name of "ye university" referred to near the end of the School Law of 1647? When and where was it founded?

_____

_____

12. The School Law of 1647 directs that "grammer" schools be established. What are these types of schools called today?

_____

13. Both of the laws speak of masters and apprentices. Look up information on the apprentice system of colonial America and explain it briefly below.

_____

_____

_____

_____

14. Why are these documents important to the history of
    education in the United States?

    _____

    _____

    _____

15. What part do state governments and the federal govern-
    ment play in education today?

    _____

    _____

    _____

    _____

    _____

    _____

THE BLOUDY TENENT OF PERSECUTION
by Roger Williams

1644

Religious nonconformist Roger Williams fled Massachusetts and established the city of Providence, Rhode Island, in 1636. Afterwards, he set down his theories about the separation of church and state in The Bloudy Tenent of Persecution.

First, that the blood of so many hundred thousand souls of Protestants and Papists, spilt in the wars of present and former ages, for their respective consciences, is not required nor accepted by Jesus Christ the Prince of Peace.

Secondly, pregnant scriptures and arguments are throughout the work proposed against the doctrine of persecution for cause of conscience.

Thirdly, satisfactory answers are given to scriptures, and objections produced by Mr. Calvin, Beza, Mr. Cotton, and the ministers of New English churches and others former and later, tending to prove the doctrine of persecution for cause of conscience.

Fourthly, the doctrine of persecution for cause of conscience is proved guilty of all the blood of the souls crying for vengeance under the altar.

Fifthly, all civil states with their officers of justice in their respective constitutions and administrations are proved essentially civil, and therefore not judges, governors, or defenders of the spiritual or Christian state and worship.

Sixthly, it is the will and command of God that (since the coming of his Son the Lord Jesus) a permission of the most paganish, Jewish, Turkish, or antichristian consciences and worships, be granted to all men in all nations and countries; and they are only to be fought against with that sword which is only (in soul matters) able to conquer, to wit, the sword of God's spirit, the Word of God.

Seventhly, the state of the Land of Israel, the kings and people thereof in peace and war, is proved figurative and ceremonial, and no pattern nor president for any kingdom or civil state in the world to follow.

Eighthly, God requireth not a uniformity of religion to be enacted and enforced in any civil state; which enforced uniformity (sooner or later) is the greatest occasion of civil war, ravishing of conscience, persecution of Christ Jesus in his servants, and of the hypocrisy and destruction of millions of souls.

Ninthly, in holding an enforced uniformity of religion in a civil state, we must necessarily disclaim our desires and hopes of the Jew's conversion to Christ.

Tenthly, an enforced uniformity of religion throughout a nation or civil state, confounds the civil and religious, denies the principles of Christianity and civility, and that Jesus Christ is come in the flesh.

Eleventhly, the permission of other consciences and worships than a state professeth only can (according to God) procure a firm and lasting peace (good assurance being taken according to the wisdom of the civil state for uniformity of civil obedience from all forts).

Twelfthly, lastly, true civility and Christianity may both flourish in a state or kingdom, notwithstanding the permission of divers and contrary consciences, either of Jew or Gentile . . .

First, the proper means whereby the civil power may and should attain its end are only political, and principally these five.

First, the erecting and establishing what form of civil government may seem in wisdom most meet, according to general rules of the world, and state of the people.

Secondly, the making, publishing, and establishing of wholesome civil laws, not only such as concern civil justice, but also the free passage of true religion; for outward civil peace ariseth and is maintained from them both, from the latter as well as from the former.

Civil peace cannot stand entire, where religion is corrupted (2 Chron. 15. 3. 5. 6; and Judges 8). And yet such laws, though conversant about religion, may still be counted civil laws, as, on the contrary, an oath doth still remain religious though conversant about civil matters.

Thirdly, election and appointment of civil officers to see execution to those laws.

Fourthly, civil punishments and rewards of transgressors and observers of these laws.

Fifthly, taking up arms against the enemies of civil peace.

Secondly, the means whereby the church may and should attain her ends are only ecclesiastical, which are chiefly five.

First, setting up that form of church government only of which Christ hath given them a pattern in his Word.

Secondly, acknowledging and admitting of no lawgiver in the church but Christ and the publishing of His laws.

Thirdly, electing and ordaining of such officers only, as Christ hath appointed in his Word.

Fourthly, to receive into their fellowship them that are approved and inflicting spiritual censures against them that offend.

Fifthly, prayer and patience in suffering any evil from them that be without, who disturb their peace.

So that magistrates, as magistrates, have no power of setting up the form of church government, electing church officers, punishing with church censures, but to see that the church does her duty herein. And on the other side, the churches as churches, have no power (though as members of the commonwealth they may have power) of erecting or altering forms of civil government, electing of civil officers, inflicting civil punishments (not on persons excommunicate) as by deposing magistrates from their civil authority, or withdrawing the hearts of the people against them, to their laws, no more than to discharge wives, or children, or servants, from due obedience to their husbands, parents, or masters; or by taking up arms against their magistrates, though he persecute them for conscience: for though members of churches who are public officers also of the civil state may suppress by force the violence of usurpers, as Iehoiada did Athaliah, yet this they do not as members of the church but as officers of the civil state.

THE BLOUDY TENENT OF PERSECUTION
by Roger Williams

1644

Facts and Concepts

1. In your own words, state what Williams means by the phrase "persecution for cause of conscience."

   _____

   _____

2. In the second paragraph, what does Williams say that he will do?

   _____

   _____

3. Read the fifth paragraph and answer the following questions.

   a. Look up the word "civil" in a dictionary or history book and write down its definition.

   _____

   _____

   b. In your own words, state the main idea of this paragraph.

   _____

   _____

   _____

4. Give a quotation from the sixth paragraph to show that Williams supports toleration for all religions.

   _____

   _____

   _____

   _____

5. According to the eighth paragraph, what are the conse-
quences of enforcing religious uniformity?

_____

_____

_____

_____

6. What does Williams mean when he says in the tenth
paragraph that uniformity of religion "confounds the civil
and religious"?

_____

_____

7. According to the eleventh paragraph, what is a benefit of
allowing other religions besides a state religion into a
colony?

_____

_____

8. Read the section of the document that begins, "*First,* the
proper means . . . " and answer the following questions.

a. List what Williams believes to be the five proper
civil powers.

_____

_____

_____

_____

b. Give a quotation showing why Williams favors making some laws about religion.

_____

_____

_____

9. Read the section of the document that begins, "*Secondly, the means whereby . . .* " and answer the following questions.

a. Look up "ecclesiastical" and write down its meaning.

_____

b. What does Williams mean when he says that "the means whereby the church may and should attain her ends are only ecclesiastical, . . . "?

_____

_____

c. List the five ecclesiastical powers that Williams says the church should have.

_____

_____

_____

_____

_____

10. Give a quotation from the last paragraph showing that Williams believed that the church should not interfere in civil affairs and that the civil government should not interfere in church affairs.

_____

_____

_____

_____

II. For Further Understanding

11. Name two American colonies that granted religious toleration before the American Revolution.

_____

12. Like Roger Williams, Anne Hutchinson was a religious leader who was banished from Massachusetts and went to live in Rhode Island. Look up information on Anne Hutchinson and write a paragraph about her religious and political activities.

_____

_____

_____

_____

_____

_____

_____

_____

13. Which amendment to the U.S. Constitution grew out of the idea of religious toleration in which Williams believed?

_____

MARYLAND TOLERATION ACT

1649

On the order of Lord Baltimore, the Toleration Act was passed in 1649 to guarantee religious freedom in Maryland. Although some problems developed between various Christian groups in the colony, Maryland became known for its policy of toleration.

Fforasmuch as in a well governed and Christian Common Wealth matters concerning Religion and the honor of God ought in the first place to bee taken, into serious consideration and endeavoured to bee settled. Be it therefore . . . enacted . . . That whatsoever person or persons within this Province . . . shall from henceforth blaspheme God, . . . or shall deny our Saviour Jesus Christ to bee the sonne of God, or shall deny the holy Trinity the ffather sonne and holy Ghost, or the Godhead of any of the said Three persons of the Trinity or the Unity of the Godhead . . . shall be punished with death and confiscation or forfeiture of all his or her lands . . .

And whereas the inforceing of the conscience in matters of Religion hath frequently fallen out to be of dangerous Consequence in those commonwealthes where it hath been practised, And for the more quiett and peaceable governement of this Province, and the better to preserve mutuall Love and amity amongst the Inhabitants thereof. Be it Therefore . . . enacted (except as in this present Act is before Declared and sett forth) that noe person or persons whatsoever within this Province, or the Islands, Ports, Harbors, Creekes, or havens thereunto belonging professing to believe in Jesus Christ, shall from henceforth bee any waies troubled, Molested or discountenanced for

or in respect of his or her religion nor in the free exercise thereof within this Province or the Islands thereunto belonging nor any way compelled to the beleife or exercise of any other Religion against his or her consent, soe as they be not unfaithful to the Lord Proprietary, or molest or conspire against the civill Government established or to bee established in this Province under him or his heires. And that all & every person and persons that shall presume Contrary to this Act and the true intent and meaning thereof directly or indirectly either in person or estate willfully to wronge disturbe trouble or molest any person whatsoever within this Province professing to believe in Jesus Christ for or in respect of his or her religion or the free exercise thereof within this Province other than is provided for in this Act that such person or persons soe offending, shalbe compelled to pay trebble damages to the party soe wronged or molested, and for every such offence shall also forfeit 20^S sterling in money or the value thereof . . . Or if the parties soe offending as aforesaid shall refuse or bee unable to recompense the party soe wronged, or to satisfy such ffyne or forfeiture, then such offender shalbe severely punished by publick whipping & imprisonment during the pleasure of the Lord proprietary, or his Leiuetenant or cheife Governor of this Province for the tyme being without baile or maineprise . . . .

MARYLAND TOLERATION ACT

1649

I. **Facts and Concepts**

1. Look up the words "confiscate" and "forfeit" in a dictionary or history book and write down their definitions.

   _____

   _____

   _____

2. What four things are forbidden in the first paragraph of this document?

   _____

   _____

   _____

   _____

   _____

3. What three reasons are given for granting religious toleration in the second paragraph?

   _____

   _____

   _____

   _____

4. Quote the phrase from the document in which religious freedom is granted.

   _____

   _____

   _____

   _____

5. What did a person have to profess to be granted toleration?

   _____

6. What two civil rules did the colonists have to obey in order to be granted toleration?

_____

_____

7. What were the two possible punishments for denying religious freedom to someone?

_____

_____

_____

8. Find and explain in your own words the contradiction between the first and second paragraphs of this document about the idea of toleration. What does this contradiction tell you?

_____

_____

_____

_____

_____

_____

_____

_____

_____

For Further Understanding

9. For whom was the colony of Maryland named?

_____

_____

10. Why did Lord Baltimore believe that the Toleration Act
    was important?

    _____

    _____

    _____

11. What two religious groups clashed in Maryland, despite the
    Toleration Act?

    _____

12. Why was Maryland's concept of religious toleration unusual
    for the time in which it was written?

    _____

    _____

    _____

    _____

RHODE ISLAND COLONIAL CHARTER

1663

The 1663 Rhode Island Charter was the second granted to the colony. It established a government and upheld the separation of church and state. This charter was kept in force until 1842, when a state constitution was adopted.

THE CHARTER
OF
THE GOVERNOR AND
COMPANY OF THE ENGLISH
COLONY OF
RHODE ISLAND AND
PROVIDENCE PLANTATIONS
IN NEW ENGLAND,
IN AMERICA.
1663

CHARLES THE SECOND, by the grace of God, 1663. King of England, Scotland, France and Ireland, Defender of the Faith, &c., to all to whome these presents shall come, greeting: Now know yee, that wee beinge willinge to encourage the hopefull undertakeinge of oure sayd loyall and loveinge subjects, and to secure them in the free exercise and enjoyment of all theire civill and religious rights, appertaining to them, as our loveinge subjects; and to preserve unto them that libertye, in the true Christian ffaith and worshipp of God, which they have sought with soe much travaill, and with peaceable myndes, and loyall subjectione to our royall progenitors and ourselves, to enjoye; and because some of the people and inhabitants of the same colonie cannot, in theire private opinions, conforme to the publique exercise of religion, according to the litturgy, formes and ceremonyes of the Church of England, or take or subscribe the oaths and articles made and established in that behalfe; and for that the same, by reason of the remote distances of those places, will (as we hope) bee noe breach of the unitie and uniformitie established in this nation: Have therefore thought ffit, and doe hereby publish, graunt, ordeyne and declare, That our royall will and pleasure is, that noe person within the sayd colonye, at any tyme hereafter, shall bee any wise molested, punished, disquieted, or all in question, for any differences in opinione in matters of religion, and doe not actually disturb the civill peace of our sayd colony; but that all and everye person and persons may, from tyme to tyme, and at all tymes hereafter, freelye and fully have and enjoye his and theire owne judgments and consciences, in matters of religious concernments, throughout the tract of lande hereafter mentioned; they behaving themselves peaceablie and quietlie, and not useinge this libertie to lycentiousnesse and profanenesse, nor to the civill injurye or outward disturbeance of others; any lawe, statute, or clause, therein contayned, or to be contayned, usage or custome of this realme, to the contrary hereof, in any wise, notwithstanding. And that they may bee in the better capacity to defend themselves, in theire just rights and libertyes against all the enemies of the Christian ffaith, and others, in all respects, wee have further thought fit, and at the humble petition of the persons aforesayd are gratiously pleased to declare, That they shall have and enjoye the benefitt of our late act of indemnity and ffree pardon, as the rest of our subjects in other our dominions and territoryes have; and to create and make them a bodye politique or corporate, with the powers and privileges hereinafter mentioned. And accordingely our will and pleasure is, and of our especiall grace, certaine knowledge, and meere motion, wee have ordeyned, constituted and declared, and by these presents, for us, our heires and successors, doe ordeyne, constitute and declare, That they, the sayd William Brenton, William Codington, Nicholas Easton, Benedict Arnold, William Boulston, John Porter, Samuell Gorton, John Smith, John Weekes, Roger Williams, Thomas Olneye, Gregorie Dexter, John Cogeshall, Joseph Clarke, Randall Holden, John Greene, John Roome, William Dyre, Samuell Wildbore, Richard Tew, William Ffeild, Thomas Harris, James Barker,_____Rainsborrow, _____ Williams, and John Nickson, and all such others as now are, or hereafter shall bee admitted and made ffree of the company and societie of our collonie of Providence Plantations, in the Narragansett Bay, in New-England, shall bee, from tyme to tyme, and forever hereafter, a bodie corporate and politique, in ffact and name, by the name of The Governor and Company of the English Collonie of Rhode-Island and Providence Plantations in New-England, in America.

RHODE ISLAND COLONIAL CHARTER
1663

Facts and Concepts

1. Which king of England granted Rhode Island this charter?

    _____

2. In what year was this charter granted?

    _____

3. What was the "hopefull undertakeinge" that the colonists
    had begun and the king wished to encourage in the
    New World?

    _____

    _____

4. Quote the phrase from the early part of the document
    showing that the king was aware of the Rhode Island
    colonists' quest for religious freedom.

    _____

    _____

    _____

5. According to the charter, why would this grant of religious
    freedom not affect the Church of England?

    _____

    _____

6. Quote the lines from the document by which the king officially grants religious freedom to the inhabitants of Rhode Island.

_____

_____

_____

_____

_____

_____

_____

_____

7. List two restrictions on this charter's grant of religious freedom.

_____

_____

_____

_____

8. Quote the phrase by which the king established a civil government for Rhode Island.

_____

_____

_____

_____

For Further Understanding

9. How long was the time period between the establishment of the first settlement in Rhode Island and the granting of this charter?

_____

10. Who founded the first settlement in Rhode Island? Why did he found it?

_____

_____

_____

_____

11. Briefly explain the significance of this document to U.S. history.

_____

_____

_____

_____

HABEAS CORPUS AMENDMENT ACT

1679

The English Parliament passed the Habeas Corpus Amendment Act in 1679. Although it did not introduce any new ideas, it strengthened existing laws and secured the rights of prisoners and all English citizens. These ideas were later incorporated as a basic part of the U.S. political system.

Whereas great delays have been used by sheriffs, gaolers and other officers to whose custody any of the King's subjects have been committed for criminal or supposed criminal matters in making returns of writs of *habeas corpus* to them directed, . . . contrary to their duty and the known law of the land, whereby many of the King's subjects have been and hereafter may be long detained in prison in such cases where by law they are bailable, to their great charge and vexation. For the prevention whereof . . . be it enacted . . . that whensoever any person or persons shall bring any *habeas corpus* directed unto any sheriff or sheriff's gaoler, minister or other persons whatsoever for any person in his or their custody . . . the said officer or officers . . . shall within three days after the service thereof as aforesaid (unless the commitment aforesaid was for treason or felony plainly and specially expressed in the warrant of commitment) . . . bring or cause to be brought the body of the party so committed . . . before the lord chancellor, or lord keeper of the Great Seal of England for the time being, or the judges or barons of the said court from whence the said writ shall issue or . . . is made returnable, . . . and shall likewise then certify the true causes of his detainer or imprisonment . . .

II. And to the intent that no sheriff, gaoler or other officer may pretend ignorance of the import of any such writ, be it enacted . . . that all such writs shall be marked in this manner, *per statutum tricesimo primo Caroli Secundi regis,* and shall be signed by the person that awards the same.

And if any person or persons shall be or stand committed or detained as aforesaid for any crime, unless for treason or felony, . . . in the vacation time and out of term, it shall and may be lawful to and for the person or persons so committed . . . to appeal or complain to the lord chancellor or lord keeper or any of his Majesty's justices . . . and the said lord chancellor . . . [is] hereby authorised and required . . . to award and grant a *habeas corpus* . . . And upon service thereof . . . the officer . . . in whose custody the party is so committed or detained shall within the times respectively before limited bring such prisoner . . . before the said lord chancellor . . . And thereupon within two days after the party shall be brought before them the said lord chancellor . . . shall discharge the said prisoner from his imprisonment, taking his or their recognisance . . . for his or their appearance in the court of King's Bench the term following, or at the next assizes, sessions or general gaol-delivery of and for such county, city or place where the commitment was . . . as the case shall require; . . . unless it shall appear . . . that the party so committed is detained . . . for such matters or offences for the which by the law the prisoner is not bailable . . .

VI. Provided always . . . that if any person or persons shall be committed for high treason or felony . . . [and] upon his prayer or petition in open court the first week of the term or the first day of the sessions of oyer and terminer or general gaol-delivery to be brought to his trial, shall not be indicted some time in the next term . . . after such commitments, it shall and may be lawful to and for the judges . . . to set at liberty the prisoner upon bail, unless it appear . . . upon oath that the witnesses for the King could not be produced the same term . . . And if any person or persons committed as aforesaid . . . shall not be indicted and tried the second term . . . after his commitment . . . he shall be discharged from his imprisonment.

VII. Provided always that nothing in this Act shall extend to discharge out of prison any person charged in debt, or other action or with process in any civil cause . . .

VIII. Provided always . . . that if any person or persons, subjects of this realm, shall be committed to any prison or in custody of any officer or officers whatsoever for any criminal or supposed criminal matter, that the said person shall not be removed from the said prison and custody into the custody of any other officer or officers unless it be by *habeas corpus* or some other legal writ . . .

X. And be it enacted . . . that a *habeas corpus* . . . may be directed and run into any country palatine, the Cinque Ports or other privileged places within the kingdom of England, dominion of Wales or town of Berwick-upon-Tweed, and the islands of Jersey or Guernsey, any law or usage to the contrary notwithstanding.

XI. And for preventing illegal imprisonments in prisons beyond the seas, be it further enacted . . . that no subject of this realm . . . shall or may be sent prisoner into Scotland, Ireland, Jersey, Guernsey, Tangier, or into any parts, garrisons, islands or places beyond the seas which are or at any time hereafter shall be within or without the dominions of his Majesty, his heirs or successors, and that every such imprisonment is hereby enacted and adjudged to be illegal . . .

HABEAS CORPUS AMENDMENT ACT

1679

I. Facts and Concepts

1. Look up the term "habeas corpus" in a dictionary or history book and write down its meaning.

_____

_____

_____

2. Read the first paragraph of the document and answer the following questions.

   a. Look up the words "gaol" and "gaoler" and write down their meanings.

   _____

   _____

   b. According to this paragraph, what had sheriffs and gaolers delayed in doing?

   _____

   _____

   c. How quickly does this document require a sheriff or gaoler to respond to a writ of habeas corpus?

   _____

   d. Where must a sheriff or gaoler take a prisoner upon the presentation of a writ of habeas corpus?

   _____

   _____

   _____

   e. What has to be explained to a court when a prisoner is brought there on a writ of habeas corpus?

   _____

   _____

f. What two types of crimes are exempted from the requirements in this paragraph?

_____

3. Read Section II and answer the following questions.

a. To whom may a prisoner appeal for a writ of habeas corpus if the regular courts are not in session?

_____

_____

b. Look up the word "recognisance" (also spelled "recognizance") and write down its definition.

_____

_____

_____

c. What does the document mean when it discusses releasing a prisoner and "taking his ... recognisance ... "?

_____

_____

4. Read Section VI and answer the following questions.

a. This section applies to what two types of crimes?

_____

b. Look up the phrase "oyer and terminer" and write down its definition.

_____

_____

c. Look up the word "indict" and write down its definition.

_____

d. What must be done with prisoners who are not indicted and tried by the second court term after they are imprisoned?

_____

_____

5. According to Section VIII, what is the only condition under which a prisoner can be removed from a prison into the custody of another officer of the law?

_____

_____

6. In what way does Section XI prevent the imprisonment of criminals in colonies acquired by England after the passage of this act? Give a quotation to support your answer.

_____

_____

_____

_____

II. For Further Understanding

7. Under what English king was this act passed?

_____

8. What country began as a British penal colony to which prisoners were transported for life as punishment?

_____

9. Quote the part of the U.S. Constitution that preserves the right of habeas corpus to U.S. citizens. (Hint: See Article I, Section 9 of the Constitution.)

_____

_____

_____

10. Which of the amendments to the Constitution guarantees the right to reasonable bail in cases in which bail is allowed?

_____

11. How does the right of habeas corpus protect the right of every citizen, not just criminals?

_____

_____

_____

ENGLISH BILL OF RIGHTS

1689

The English Bill of Rights is one of the most important documents in that country's history. Although it did not establish any new rights, it explicitly stated and demanded recognition of the basic rights of English people. It defined the roles of the monarch and of Parliament, laying a foundation for English government that carried over into the American colonies.

An Act Declaring the Rights
and Liberties
of the Subject and
Settling the Succession
of the Crown

Whereas the Lords Spiritual and Temporal and Commons assembled at Westminster, lawfully, fully and freely representing all the estates of the people of this realm, did upon the thirteenth day of February in the year of our Lord one thousand six hundred eighty-eight present unto their Majesties, then called and known by the names and style of William and Mary, prince and princess of Orange, being present in their proper persons, a certain declaration in writing made by the said Lords and Commons in the words following, viz.:

Whereas the late King James the Second, by the assistance of divers evil counsellors, judges and ministers employed by him, did endeavour to subvert and extirpate the Protestant religion and the laws and liberties of this kingdom;

By assuming and exercising a power of dispensing with and suspending of laws and the execution of laws without consent of Parliament;

By committing and prosecuting divers worthy prelates for humbly petitioning to be excused from concurring to the said assumed power;

By issuing and causing to be executed a commission under the great seal for erecting a court called the Court of Commissioners for Ecclesiastical Causes;

By levying money for and to the use of the Crown by pretence of prerogative for other time and in other manner than the same was granted by Parliament;

By raising and keeping a standing army within this kingdom in time of peace without consent of Parliament, and quartering soldiers contrary to law;

By causing several good subjects being Protestants to be disarmed at the same time when papists were both armed and employed contrary to law;

By violating the freedom of election of members to serve in Parliament;

By prosecutions in the Court of King's Bench for matters and causes cognizable only in Parliament, and by divers other arbitrary and illegal courses;

And whereas of late years partial corrupt and unqualified persons have been returned and served on juries in trials, and particularly divers jurors in trials for high treason which were not freeholders;

And excessive bail hath been required of persons committed in criminal cases to elude the benefit of the laws made for the liberty of the subjects;

And excessive fines have been imposed;

And illegal and cruel punishments inflicted;

And several grants and promises made of fines and forfeitures before any conviction or judgment against the persons upon whom the same were to be levied;

All which are utterly and directly contrary to the known laws and statutes and freedom of this realm;

And whereas the said late King James the Second having abdicated the government and the throne being thereby vacant, his Highness the prince of Orange (whom it hath pleased Almighty God to make the glorious instrument of delivering this kingdom from popery and arbitrary power) did (by the advice of the Lords Spiritual and Temporal and divers principal persons of the Commons) cause letters to be written to the Lords Spiritual and Temporal being Protestants, and other letters to the several counties, cities, universities, boroughs and cinque ports, for the choosing of such persons to represent them as were of right to be sent to Parliament, to meet and sit at Westminster upon the two and twentieth day of January in this year one thousand six hundred eighty and eight, in order to such an establishment as that their religion, laws and liberties might not again be in danger of being subverted, upon which letters elections having been accordingly made;

And thereupon the said Lords Spiritual and Temporal and Commons, pursuant to their respective letters and elections, being now assembled in a full and free representative of this nation, taking into their most serious consideration the best means for attaining the ends aforesaid, do in the first place (as their ancestors in like case have usually done) for the vindicating and asserting their ancient rights and liberties declare

That the pretended power of suspending of laws or the execution of laws by regal authority without consent of Parliament is illegal;

That the pretended power of dispensing with laws or the execution of laws by regal authority, as it hath been assumed and exercised of late, is illegal;

That the commission for erecting the late Court of Commissioners for Ecclesiastical Causes, and all other commissions and courts of like nature, are illegal and pernicious;

That levying money for or to the use of the Crown by pretence of prerogative, without grant of Parliament, for longer time, or in other manner than the same is or shall be granted, is illegal;

That it is the right of the subjects to petition the king, and all commitments and prosecutions for such petitioning are illegal;

That the raising or keeping a standing army within the kingdom in time of peace, unless it be with consent of Parliament, is against law;

That the subjects which are Protestants may have arms for their defence suitable to their conditions and as allowed by law;

That election of members of Parliament ought to be free;

That the freedom of speech and debates or proceedings in Parliament ought not to be impeached or questioned in any court or place out of Parliament;

That excessive bail ought not to be required, nor excessive fines imposed, nor cruel and unusual punishments inflicted;

That jurors ought to be duly impanelled and returned, and jurors which pass upon men in trials for high treason ought to be freeholders;

That all grants and promises of fines and forfeitures of particular persons before conviction are illegal and void;

And that for redress of all grievances, and for the amending, strengthening and preserving of the laws, Parliaments ought to be held frequently.

And they do claim, demand and insist upon all and singular the premises as their undoubted rights and liberties, and that no declarations, judgments, doings or proceedings to the prejudice of the people in any of the said premises ought in any wise to be drawn hereafter into consequence or example; to which demand of their rights they are particularly encouraged by the declaration of his Highness the prince of Orange as being the only means for obtaining a full redress and remedy therein. Having therefore an entire confidence that his said Highness the prince of Orange will perfect the deliverance so far advanced by him, and will still preserve them from the violation of their rights which they have here asserted, and from all other attempts upon their religion, rights and liberties, the said Lords Spiritual and Temporal and Commons assembled at Westminster do resolve that William and Mary, prince and princess of Orange, be and be declared king and queen of England, France and Ireland and the dominions thereunto belonging, to hold the crown and royal dignity of the said kingdoms and dominions to them, the said prince and princess, during their lives and the life of the survivor of them, and that the sole and full exercise of the regal power be only in and executed by the said prince of Orange in the names of the said prince and princess during their joint lives, and after their deceases the said crown and royal dignity of the said kingdoms and dominions to be to the heirs of the body of the said princess, and for default of such issue to the Princess Anne of Denmark and

the heirs of her body, and for default of such issue to the heirs of the body of the said prince of Orange. And the Lords Spiritual and Temporal and Commons do pray the said prince and princess to accept the same accordingly.

And that the oaths hereafter mentioned be taken by all persons of whom the oaths of allegiance and supremacy might be required by law, instead of them; and that the said oaths of allegiance and supremacy be abrogated.

I, A.B., do sincerely promise and swear that I will be faithful and bear true allegiance to their Majesties King William and Queen Mary. So help me God.

I, A.B., do swear that I do from my heart abhor, detest and abjure as impious and heretical this damnable doctrine and position, that princes excommunicated or deprived by the Pope or any authority of the see of Rome may be deposed or murdered by their subjects or any other whatsoever. And I do declare that no foreign prince, person, prelate, state or potentate hath or ought to have any jurisdiction, power, superiority, pre-eminence or authority, ecclesiastical or spiritual, within this realm. So help me God.

Upon which their said Majesties did accept the crown and royal dignity of the kingdoms of England, France and Ireland, and the dominions thereunto belonging, according to the resolution and desire of the said Lords and Commons contained in the said declaration. And thereupon their Majesties were pleased that the said Lords Spiritual and Temporal and Commons, being the two Houses of Parliament, should continue to sit, and with their Majesties' royal concurrence make effectual provision for the settlement of the religion, laws and liberties of this kingdom, so that the same for the future might not be in danger again of being subverted, to which the said Lords Spiritual and Temporal and Commons did agree, and proceed to act accordingly. Now in pursuance of the premises the said Lords Spiritual and Temporal and Commons in Parliament assembled, for the ratifying, confirming and establishing the said declaration and the articles, clauses, matters and things therein contained by the force of a law made in due form by authority of Parliament, do pray that it may be declared and enacted that all and singular the rights and liberties asserted and claimed in the said declaration are the true, ancient and indubitable rights and liberties of the people of this kingdom, and so shall be esteemed, allowed, adjudged, deemed and taken to be; and that all and every the particulars aforesaid shall be firmly and strictly holden and observed as they are expressed in the said declaration, and all officers and ministers whatsoever shall serve their Majesties and their successors according to the same in all times to come. And the said Lords Spiritual and Temporal and Commons, seriously considering how it hath pleased Almighty God in his marvellous providence and merciful goodness to this nation to provide and preserve their said Majesties' royal persons most happily to reign over us upon the throne of their ancestors, for which they render unto him from the bottom of their hearts their humblest thanks and praises, do truly, firmly, assuredly and in the sincerity of their hearts think, and do hereby recognize, acknowledge and declare, that King James the Second having abdicated the government, and their Majesties having accepted the crown and royal dignity as aforesaid, their said Majesties did become, were, are and of right ought to be by the laws of this realm our sovereign liege lord and lady, king and queen of England, France and Ireland and the dominions thereunto belonging, in and to whose princely persons the royal state, crown and dignity of the said realms with all honours, styles, titles, regalities, prerogatives, powers, jurisdictions and authorities to the same belonging and appertaining are most fully, rightfully and entirely invested and incorporated, united and annexed. And for preventing all questions and divisions in this realm by reason of any pretended titles to the crown, and for preserving a certainty in the succession thereof, in and upon which the unity, peace, tranquillity and safety in this nation doth under God wholly consist and depend, the said Lords Spiritual and Temporal and Commons do beseech their Majesties that it may be enacted, established and declared, that the crown and regal government of the said kingdoms and dominions, with all and singular the premises thereunto belonging and appertaining, shall be and continue to their said Majesties and the survivor of them during their lives and the life of the survivor of them, and that the entire, perfect and full exercise of the regal power and government be only in and executed by his Majesty in the names of both their Majesties during their joint lives; and after their deceases the said crown and premises shall be and remain to the heirs of the body of her Majesty, and for default of such issue to her Royal Highness the Princess Anne of Denmark and the heirs of her body, and for default of such issue to the heirs of the body of his said Majesty; and thereunto the said Lords Spiritual and Temporal and Commons do in the name of all the people aforesaid most humbly and faithfully submit themselves, their heirs and posterities for ever, and do faithfully promise that they will stand to, maintain and defend their said Majesties, and also the limitation and succession of the crown herein specified and contained, to the utmost of their powers with their lives and estates against all persons whatsoever that shall attempt anything to the contrary. And whereas it hath been found by experience that it is inconsistent with the safety and welfare of this Protestant kingdom to be governed by a popish prince, or by any king or queen marrying a papist, the said Lords Spiritual and Temporal and Commons do further pray that it may be enacted, that all and every person and persons that is, are or shall be reconciled to or shall hold communion with the see or Church of Rome, or shall profess the popish religion, or shall marry a papist, shall be excluded and be for ever incapable to inherit, possess or enjoy the crown and government of this realm and Ireland and the dominions thereunto belonging or any part of the same, or to have, use or exercise any regal power, authority or jurisdiction within the same; and in all and every such case or cases the people of these realms shall be and are hereby absolved of their allegiance; and the said crown and government shall from time to time descend to and be enjoyed by such person or persons being Protestants as should have inherited and enjoyed the same in case the said person or persons so reconciled, holding communion or professing or marrying as aforesaid were naturally dead; and that every king and queen of this realm who at any time hereafter shall come to and succeed in the imperial crown of this kingdom shall on the first day of the meeting of the first Parliament next after his or her coming to the crown, sitting in his or her throne in the House of Peers in the presence of the Lords and Commons therein assembled, or at his or her coronation before such person or persons who shall administer the coronation oath to him or her at the time of his or her taking the said oath (which shall first happen), make, subscribe and audibly repeat the declaration mentioned in the statute made in the thirtieth year of the reign of King Charles the Second entituled, *An Act for the more effectual preserving the king's person and government by disabling papists from sitting in either House of Parliament*. But if it shall happen that such king or queen upon his or her succession to the crown of this realm shall be under the age of twelve years, then every such king or queen shall make, subscribe and audibly repeat the said declaration at his or her coronation or the first day of the meeting of the first Parliament as aforesaid which shall first happen after such king or queen shall have attained the said age of twelve years. All which their Majesties are contented and pleased shall be declared, enacted and established by authority of this present Parliament, and shall stand, remain and be the law of this realm for ever; and the same are by their said Majesties, by and with the advice and consent of the

Lords Spiritual and Temporal and Commons in Parliament assembled and by the authority of the same, declared, enacted and established accordingly.

II. And be it further declared and enacted by the authority aforesaid, that from and after this present session of Parliament no dispensation by *non obstante* of or to any statute or any part thereof shall be allowed, but that the same shall be held void and of no effect, except a dispensation be allowed of in such statute, and except in such cases as shall be specially provided for by one or more bill or bills to be passed during this present session of Parliament.

III. Provided that no charter or grant or pardon granted before the three and twentieth day of October in the year of our Lord one thousand six hundred eighty-nine shall be any ways impeached or invalidated by this Act, but that the same shall be and remain of the same force and effect in law and no other than as if this Act had never been made.

ENGLISH BILL OF RIGHTS
1689

I. Facts and Concepts

1. Who became the king and queen of England just before this document was written?

    _____

2. Who wrote this document and presented it to the king and queen?

    _____

3. Read the second paragraph and answer the following questions.

    a. Look up the words "subvert" and "extirpate" in a dictionary and write down their definitions.

    _____

    _____

    b. What three things is the king accused of trying to "subvert and extirpate"?

    _____

    _____

    _____

4. What is the king accused of in the third paragraph?

    _____

    _____

5. According to the paragraph that begins "By levying money . . . ," what group of people did the king not consult in raising money?

    _____

6. What two things are protested in the paragraph that begins "By raising and keeping . . . "?

    _____

    _____

7. Read the paragraph that begins "By causing several good subjects . . . " and answer the following questions.

   a. Look up the word "papist" and write down its meaning.

_____

_____

   b. What were papists allowed to do that Protestants could not do?

_____

_____

8. List the four offenses mentioned in the paragraph that begins "And whereas of late years . . . ," and the three paragraphs that follow it.

_____

_____

_____

9. In your own words, state the main idea of the paragraph that begins "All which are . . . "

_____

_____

10. Read the paragraph that begins "And whereas the said . . . " and answer the following questions.

   a. Look up the word "abdicate" and explain what the king had done when he "abdicated the government."

_____

   b. What was the purpose of the letters written by William of Orange that are mentioned in this paragraph?

_____

_____

11. The authors of this document make several declarations that are meant to correct the grievances listed in the document. Read these declarations carefully and choose the five you consider to be the most important. In your own words, explain why you believe they are the most significant.

_____

_____

_____

_____

_____

_____

_____

_____

_____

_____

_____

_____

_____

12. Read the paragraph that begins "And they do claim . . ." and explain what the phrase "no declarations . . . to the prejudice of the people in any of the said premises ought in any wise to be drawn hereafter into consequence or example . . ." means.

_____

_____

_____

_____

13. Explain in your own words what the new king and queen had to declare in the paragraph that begins "I, A.B., do swear that I do . . ."

_____

_____

_____

_____

14. Read the paragraph that begins "Upon which their said Majesties . . ." and answer the following questions.

   a. Who does this paragraph say will work together to establish laws?

   _____

   b. Why do you think that Parliament emphasizes its own powers in this paragraph?

   _____

   _____

   _____

   c. Explain in your own words why Parliament was interested in "preserving a certainty in the succession" to the English throne.

   _____

   _____

   _____

   d. What two groups of people does this paragraph prevent from becoming rulers of England?

   _____

15. Read Section II and answer the following questions.

    a. Look up the term *non obstante* and write down its meaning and significance to this section.

_____

_____

_____

    b. What were the only ways in which exceptions to laws passed by Parliament could be made?

_____

_____

_____

II. For Further Understanding

16. What religion was James II?

_____

17. What was the name of the event in which James II was deposed and William and Mary were put on the throne?

_____

18. What two branches of the U.S. government have duties similar to those of the English monarch and Parliament as described in this document?

_____

_____

19. This document says that "excessive bail ought not to be required, nor excessive fines imposed, nor cruel and unusual punishments inflicted." Quote the amendment to the U.S. Constitution that affirms these principles.

_____

_____

_____

_____

20. How does the organization of the U.S. government prevent "arbitrary and illegal" actions?

_____

_____

PENNSYLVANIA CHARTER OF PRIVILEGES

1701

William Penn, the proprietor of Pennsylvania, had very definite ideas about the way he wanted his colony to function. His plans, however, often conflicted with those of others in the colony. In the late 1600s, after many disputes, Penn finally agreed to allow the Pennsylvania Assembly to create a constitution. The result was the Pennsylvania Charter of Privileges, which remained the Pennsylvania constitution until 1776.

William Penn, Proprietary and Governor of the Province of *Pensilvania* and Territories thereunto belonging, To all to whom these Presents shall come, sendeth Greeting. Whereas King Charles *the Second,* by His Letters Patents, under the Great Seal of *England,* bearing Date the *Fourth* Day of *March,* in the Year *One Thousand Six Hundred and Eighty-one,* was graciously pleased to give and grant unto me, and my Heirs and Assigns for ever, this Province of *Pensilvania,* with divers great Powers and Jurisdictions for the well Government thereof . . .

KNOW YE THEREFORE, That for the further Well-being and good Government of the said Province, and Territories and in Pursuance of the Rights and Powers before-mentioned, I the said *William Penn* do declare, grant and confirm, unto all the Freemen, Planters and Adventurers, and other Inhabitants of this Province and Territories, these following Liberties, Franchises and Privileges, so far as in me lieth, to be held, enjoyed and kept, by the Freemen, Planters and Adventurers, and other Inhabitants of and in the said

Province and Territories thereunto annexed, for ever.

FIRST

BECAUSE no People can be truly happy, though under the greatest Enjoyment of Civil Liberties, if abridged of the Freedom of their Consciences, as to their Religious Profession and Worship: And Almighty God being the only Lord of Conscience, Father of Lights and Spirits; and the Author as well as Object of all divine Knowledge, Faith and Worship, who only doth enlighten the Minds, and persuade and convince the Understandings of People, I do hereby grant and declare, That no Person or Persons, inhabiting in this province or Territories, who shall confess and acknowledge *One* almighty God, the Creator, Upholder and Ruler of the World; and profess him or themselves obliged to live quietly under the Civil Government, shall be in any Case molested or prejudiced, in his or their Person or Estate, because of his or their conscientious Persuasion or Practice, nor be compelled to frequent or maintain any religious Worship, Place or Ministry, contrary to his or their Mind, or to do or suffer any other Act or Thing, contrary to their religious Persuasion.

AND that all Persons who also profess to believe in *Jesus Christ,* the Saviour of the World, shall be capable (notwithstanding their other Persuasions and Practices in Point of Conscience and Religion) to serve this Government in any Capacity, both legislatively and executively, he or they solemnly promising, when lawfully required, Allegiance to the King as Sovereign, and Fidelity to the

Proprietary and Governor, and taking the Attests as now established by the Law made at *New-Castle,* in the Year *One Thousand and Seven Hundred,* entitled, *An Act directing the Attests of several Officers and Ministers,* as now amended and confirmed this present Assembly.

II. For the well governing of this Province and Territories, there shall be an Assembly yearly chosen, by the Freemen thereof, to consist of *Four* Persons out of each County, of most Note for Virtue, Wisdom and Ability . . . Which Assembly shall have Power to chuse a Speaker and other their Officers; and shall be Judges of the Qualifications and Elections of their own Members; sit upon their own Adjournments; appoint Committees; prepare Bills in order to pass into Laws; impeach Criminals, and redress Grievances; and shall have all other Powers and Privileges of an Assembly, according to the Rights of the free-born Subjects of *England,* and as is usual in any of the King's Plantations in *America* . . .

III. THAT the Freemen in each respective County, at the Time and Place of Meeting for Electing their Representatives to serve in Assembly, may as often as there shall be Occasion, chuse a double Number of Persons to present to the Governor for Sheriffs and Coroners to serve for *Three* Years, if so long they behave themselves well; out of which respective Elections and Presentments, the Governor shall nominate and commissionate one for each of the said Officers, the *Third* Day after such Presentment, or else the *First* named in such Presentment, for each Office as aforesaid, shall stand and serve in that Office for the Time before

respectively limited; and in Case of Death or Default, such Vacancies shall be supplied by the Governor, to serve to the End of the said Term . . .

AND that the Justices of the respective Counties shall or may nominate and present to the Governor *Three* Persons, to serve for Clerk of the Peace for the said County, when there is a Vacancy, one of which the Governor shall commissionate within *Ten* Days after such Presentment, or else the *First* nominated shall serve in the said Office during good Behavior.

IV. THAT the Laws of this Government shall be in this Stile, viz. *By the Governor, with the Consent and Approbation of the Freemen in General Assembly met;* and shall be, after Confirmation by the Governor, forthwith recorded in the Rolls Office, and kept at *Philadelphia,* unless the Governor and Assembly shall agree to appoint another Place.

V. THAT all Criminals shall have the same Privileges of Witnesses and Council as their Prosecutors.

VI. THAT no Person or Persons shall or may, at any Time hereafter, be obliged to answer any Complaint, Matter or Thing whatsoever, relating to Property, before the Governor and Council, or in any other Place, but in ordinary Course of Justice, unless Appeals thereunto shall be hereafter by Law appointed.

VII. THAT no Person within this Government, shall be licensed by the Governor to keep an Ordinary, Tavern or House of Publick Entertainment, but such who are first recommended to him, under the Hands of the Justices of the respective Counties, signed in open Court; which Justices are and shall be hereby impowered, to suppress and forbid any Person, keeping such Publick-House as aforesaid, upon their Misbehavior, on such Penalties as the Law doth or shall direct; and to recommend others from time to time, as they shall see Occasion . . .

VIII. BUT because the Happiness of Mankind depends so much upon the Enjoying of Liberty of their Consciences as aforesaid, I do hereby solemnly declare, promise and grant, for me, my Heirs and Assigns, That the *First* Article of this Charter relating to Liberty of Conscience, and every Part and Clause therein, according to the true Intent and Meaning thereof, shall be kept and remain, without any Alteration, inviolably for ever.

AND LASTLY, I the said *William Penn,* Proprietary and Governor of the Province of *Pensilvania,* and Territories thereunto belonging, for myself, my Heirs and Assigns, have solemnly declared, granted and confirmed, and do hereby solemnly declare, grant and confirm, That neither I, my Heirs or Assigns, shall procure or do any Thing or Things whereby the Liberties in this Charter contained and expressed, nor any Part thereof, shall be infringed or broken: And if any thing shall be procured or done, by any Person or Persons, contrary to these Presents, it shall be held of no Force or Effect . . .

PENNSYLVANIA CHARTER OF PRIVILEGES

1701

Facts and Concepts

1. Who was the governor of Pennsylvania in 1701?

   _____

2. Which English king had granted Pennsylvania to this governor?

   _____

3. Read the paragraph that begins "KNOW YE THEREFORE . . . " and answer the following questions.

   a. What reason is given for granting the charter?

   _____

   _____

   b. To what persons are the privileges of the charter granted?

   _____

   c. For what period of time were the privileges granted?

   _____

4. Read the first paragraph under the section "FIRST" and answer the following questions.

   a. What important freedom is granted in this paragraph?

   _____

   b. Quote a phrase from this paragraph showing the qualifications that a person must meet to be eligible for this freedom.

   _____

   _____

   _____

5. What privilege is granted to the inhabitants of Pennsylvania in the paragraph beginning "AND that all persons . . . "?

_____

_____

6. Read Section II and answer the following questions.

a. Quote the part of this section that grants the colonists representation in their government.

_____

_____

_____

b. List six powers granted to the representative body.

_____

_____

_____

_____

_____

_____

7. Read Section III and answer the following questions.

a. The rules for selecting what two officers are described in the first paragraph of this section?

_____

b. What part do the freemen of Pennsylvania play in the election of these officers?

_____

c. For what period of time do those officers serve?

_____

d. How are vacancies filled if they occur during an officer's term?

_____

_____

e. Provisions for selecting what officer are described in the second paragraph of this section?

_____

f. Describe in your own words the manner in which this officer is chosen.

_____

_____

_____

_____

8. After reading Section IV, state in your own words why it is important that laws be written down and kept in a public place.

_____

_____

_____

_____

9. In your own words, describe the right granted to people accused of crimes in Section V.

_____

_____

10. Explain in your own words the privilege granted in Section VI.

_____

_____

_____

11. What does the proprietor of the colony guarantee to the colonists in Section VIII?

_____

_____

12. What does the last paragraph of the document guarantee?

_____

_____

II. For Further Understanding

13. What is the meaning of the name "Pennsylvania?"

_____

14. What religion was Penn? What effect did this have on his interest in religious freedom?

_____

_____

_____

_____

15. What national government body of the U.S. today closely matches the description of the assembly in Section II? Be specific in your answer.

_____

16. What amendment to the U.S. Constitution grants the same rights as those mentioned in Section V?

_____

ANSWER KEY

Magna Carta

1. John

2. This document was signed at Runnymede on June 15, 1215.

3. a. According to feudal law, a relief is a fee paid to gain the right to inherit property.

   b. A ward is a child placed under the protection of a guardian. The problem that Section 4 tries to solve is guardians of wards taking more than reasonable revenues, dues, and services from people on land belonging to wards.

   c. By forcing a widow to marry him, a person could gain the right to her deceased husband's property.

4. According to Section 9, the farmer's chattels will be taken from him, because they are sufficient to pay his debt without seizing his land or his house.

5. Section 41 guarantees that "all merchants shall be able to go out of and come into England safely and securely, and stay and travel throughout England, . . . "

6. This statement is important because it guarantees that the nobles have a voice in whether or not they will be taxed.

7. a. To amerce is to punish by arbitrarily imposing a fine.

   b. This section guarantees that no one will be amerced except in proportion to the nature of the wrong they have done.

8. Section 38 prohibits the practice of putting people to trial without witnesses.

9. a. To disseise is to take someone's property illegally.

   b. An owner could have disseised lands returned to him if they had been taken without the legal judgment of his peers.

10. Section 39 prohibits punishing people without the lawful judgment of their peers or by the law of the land.

11. Section 45 is designed to prevent the king from appointing law enforcement officials who are not qualified.

12. a. The purpose of the council is to make sure that the rights granted in the document are upheld.

b. According to Section 61, abuses are to be reported to four of the twenty-five barons. These barons will then ask the king to correct the abuse. If it is not corrected, the abuse is brought before the entire council, which will take action against the king to force him to correct it.

13. Section 63 says that the king and the barons will take an oath to promise to carry out the provisions of the document.

14. The words "we" and "our" refer to King John.

15. During his reign, King John abused his powers, increasing the military service requirements of the barons, increasing taxes without the consent of the barons, and abusing legal practices. The barons drew up the Magna Carta to correct these abuses, raised an army, and forced the king to agree to their demands.

16. An "unwritten constitution" is a set of rules and traditions followed in a country that are not set down in a specific document. The English constitution is based on tradition, custom, and the English common law. Many elements of the English constitution are contained in documents like the Magna Carta.

17. "No taxation without representation."

18. the Fourteenth Amendment

Mayflower Compact

1. A body politic is a group of people who live under an organized government. To covenant is to enter into a solemn agreement. Civil is used to describe something that applies to a citizen or a group of citizens. Ordinances are laws or regulations.

2. November 11, 1620

3. James I

4. According to the document, the Pilgrims had planned to land in northern Virginia. The area where they actually landed is now part of Massachusetts.

5. Because there are many references to God and faith in the document, answers will vary.

6. "We . . . solemnly and mutually in the Presence of God and one another, covenant and combine ourselves together . . . and by Virtue hereof do enact, constitute, and frame, such just and equal Laws, Ordinances, Acts, Constitutions, and Offices, from time to time, as shall be thought most meet and convenient for the general Good of the Colony . . ."

7. Many of the pilgrims announced during their journey that they would not recognize the jurisdiction of the Virginia Company over them when they landed in America. Pilgrim leaders believed that the Mayflower Compact was necessary so that they would have some kind of civil order in their colony.

8. The Pilgrims were members of a group called the Separatists, who refused to follow the practices of the Church of England. The Separatists were persecuted in England for their beliefs, and many of them moved to the Netherlands. They decided, however, that they wanted their children to grow up English, so established a colony of their own in America.

9. The London Company gave the Pilgrims a land grant to settle in Virginia. They did not settle there because storms blew them off course and they decided to stay where they had landed, further north on the New England coast.

10. No. The document only required the Pilgrims to submit to the authority of whatever government they established.

Petition of Right

1. The House of Lords and the House of Commons of the English Parliament.

2. a. A tallage is a tax levied on royal lands and towns. A benevolence is a compulsory tax established by a king without the consent of a parliament.

   b. The king was trying to raise money through all of the actions described in this paragraph.

   c. The main idea of this paragraph is that English people should not have to pay taxes established by the king without the consent of Parliament.

3. The main idea of Section III is that people cannot be punished in any way except by the lawful judgment of their peers.

4. Due process of law is the principle that requires governments to make legal decisions through a fair and organized process.

5. In Section V, the king is accused of allowing some of his subjects to be taken prisoner and held without cause.

6. Section VI describes how people have been required to provide housing for soldiers against their will.

7. a. Martial law is rule by military authorities.

   b. The king had used martial law to put people to death without due process of law.

8. The second paragraph of Section VII says that if the people who had been executed under martial law were guilty of capital offenses, they could have and should have been tried and executed under existing laws.

9. The purpose of Section VIII is to ask the king to correct the abuses outlined in the previous sections.

10. a. The writers of the petition are asking for rights and liberties that are already contained in the laws and statutes of England.

    b. The last sentence of the document asks that the king declare it his "royal will and pleasure" that the ministers obey the laws and statutes of England.

11. Charles I

12. He was executed during the English Revolution.

13. the Magna Carta

14. The Fifth Amendment to the U.S. Constitution guarantees the same rights as those found in Section III. It states that "no person shall be . . . deprived of life, liberty, or property, without due process of law."

15. U.S. taxes are enacted by representatives and senators in Congress, and are approved by the president. All of these officials are elected by the people of the United States.

Fundamental Orders of Connecticut

1. Windsor, Hartford, and Wethersfield

2. "we the Inhabitants and Residents of Windsor, Harteford, and Wethersfield . . . doe therefore assotiate and conioyne our selves to be as one Publike State or Commonwelth . . . "

3. a. The purpose of the Court of Election is to choose magistrates and other public officials.

   b. A magistrate is a public official who has the power to enforce laws.

c. The document stipulates that as many magistrates should be elected as are necessary, but at least six besides the governor.

d. To participate in the election of magistrates, a person must be a freeman, must have taken the oath of fidelity, and must be living within the jurisdiction of the Fundamental Orders.

4. According to Section 5, the purpose of the General Court is to make laws and deal with any other issues concerning the good of the Commonwealth.

5. According to Section 7, deputies must be freemen of the commonwealth.

6. "whatsoever other Townes shall be hereafter added to this Jurisdiction, they shall send so many deputyes as the Courte shall judge meete . . . "

7. In Section 9, the deputies are granted the power to appoint a time to meet to discuss matters of public interest and verify the results of their elections.

8. a. A majority of the freemen in the commonwealth can call a General Court if the governor and the magistrates neglect or refuse to do so.

   b. the General Courts

   c. The General Courts are granted the following seven powers: to make laws, repeal laws, grant levies, admit freemen, sell lands, try and punish courts or magistrates for crimes, and deal with any other matter concerning the good of the commonwealth.

9. The governor or moderator is granted the power to order the Court to allow free speech, to silence disorderly speakers, to call for votes on questions, and to cast tie-breaking votes.

10. a. taxes

    b. The purpose of the special committee is to determine what proportion of taxes should be paid by each town.

11. Thomas Hooker

12. Some of the settlers went in search of political and religious freedom, and others wanted to find new opportunities on the American frontier.

13. four years (1635-39)

Massachusetts School Laws

1. The problem of parents and masters neglecting to train their children in "learning and labor" is stated as the reason for this law.

2. The people who have been appointed to manage the affairs of towns are made responsible for education.

3. Fines were prescribed for people who did not carry out their duties regarding education.

4. Those responsible for education were allowed to call on parents, masters, and children, and test the children to see if they understood principles of religion and law.

5. Boys and girls were not allowed to converse with each other because this might "occasion ... wanton, dishonest, or immodest behavior; ... "

6. This document requires training in reading and in working with tools and implements.

7. The first paragraph says that children should know how to read and write so that they can read the Bible and not be deceived by people who misinterpret it.

8. This document requires townships of more than fifty households to appoint someone to teach all the children in the township to read and write.

9. The document requires towns of more than one hundred households to set up a grammar school.

10. The goal of the schools set up in townships of more than one hundred households was to prepare students to attend a university.

11. Harvard University was established in 1636 at Cambridge, Massachusetts.

12. elementary schools

13. In the apprentice system of colonial America, parents handed boys over to masters in particular trades. These boys were then called apprentices. The masters taught their trades to the apprentices, who were required to obey the masters. After a specified period of time apprentices became free workers.

14. These documents are important to the history of education in the United States because they are the first examples of laws aimed at establishing a system of public education.

15. Answers will vary because state governments and the federal government play a large role in education. In general, these governments build and fund schools, set standards of educational performance, and license teachers.

The Bloudy Tenent of Persecution

1. Williams uses the term "persecution for cause of conscience" to describe mistreating people because of their religious beliefs.

2. In the second paragraph, Williams says that he will present "scriptures and arguments . . . against the doctrine of persecution for cause of conscience."

3. a. Civil is used to describe something that applies to a citizen or a group of citizens.

   b. The main idea of this paragraph is that governments should concern themselves only with civil matters, and that church and state should remain separate.

4. "it is the will and command of God that . . . a permission of the most paganish, Jewish, Turkish, or antichristian consciences and worships, be granted to all men in all nations and countries; . . . "

5. The eighth paragraph says that requiring religious uniformity results in civil war, the "ravishing of conscience," the persecution of Jesus Christ and his servants, and the hypocrisy and destruction of millions of souls.

6. When Williams says that uniformity of religion "confounds the civil and religious," he means that it mixes the two elements, which he says should remain separate.

7. According to Williams, a benefit of allowing other religions besides a state religion into a colony is that it will assure "a firm and lasting peace."

8. a. 1. establishing a civil government
      2. passing laws concerning civil justice and religion
      3. electing and appointing civil officers to enforce laws
      4. punishing people who break laws and rewarding people who observe them
      5. using force to keep the peace, if necessary

   b. "Civil peace cannot stand entire, where religion is corrupted . . . "

9. a. Ecclesiastical means of or pertaining to a church.

b. Williams means that the church should not use civil means to attain its ends.

c. 1. to set up a church government, based on the word of Christ
2. to acknowledge no lawmaker for the church except Christ
3. to elect and ordain church officers
4. to admit members to the church and punish people who break church laws
5. to use prayer and patience against people who disturb the peace of the church

10. "magistrates, as magistrates, have no power of setting up the form of church government, ... And on the other side, the churches, as churches, have no power ... of erecting or altering forms of civil government ..."

11. Answers will vary, because most of the middle colonies granted religious toleration. Rhode Island, Pennsylvania, Delaware, and Maryland are four examples.

12. Anne Hutchinson went to Massachusetts in 1634. She was very interested in religious matters, and came into conflict with religious leaders in Massachusetts because she insisted that faith alone, not good works, was necessary for salvation. She was exiled from Massachusetts in 1639 and founded Portsmouth, Rhode Island. She and her family were massacred by Indians in New York in 1643.

13. the First Amendment

Maryland Toleration Act

1. To confiscate is to seize by authority. To forfeit is to lose or be forced to give up something because of one's actions.

2. The four things forbidden in the first paragraph of this document are blaspheming God, denying that Jesus Christ is the son of God, denying the Holy Trinity, and denying the divinity of any of the members of the Trinity.

3. Three reasons given for granting religious toleration are because the enforcement of particular beliefs has proved dangerous in some commonwealths, for the quiet and peaceable government of the colony, and to better preserve the mutual love and amity of the people of the colony.

4. "Be it Therefore ... enacted ... that noe person or persons whatsoever within this Province, ... professing to believe in Jesus Christ, shall from henceforth bee any waies troubled, Molested, or discountenanced for or in respect of his or her religion nor in the free exercise thereof within this Province ..."

5. To be granted toleration, a person had to profess a belief in Jesus Christ.

6. Two rules that a colonist had to obey to be granted toleration were: being faithful to the lord proprietary of the colony and not conspiring against the civil government of the colony.

7. The two possible punishments for denying religious freedom to someone were: being forced to pay triple damages to the wronged party and a fine of twenty shillings, or being publicly whipped and imprisoned.

8. In the second paragraph the document says that all people who profess a belief in Jesus Christ will be granted toleration. The first paragraph, however, lists a series of offenses that Christians might commit for which they could be punished with death and confiscation or forfeiture of their lands. This indicates that there were probably stricter limits on toleration than the second paragraph implies.

9. Maryland was named in honor of Queen Henrietta Maria, the wife of King Charles I of England.

10. Lord Baltimore believed that the Toleration Act was important because although he wanted the colony to allow the free exercise of Catholicism, he thought that restrictions on other Christian religions would impede its growth.

11. Despite the Toleration Act, Protestants and Catholics clashed in Maryland.

12. The Toleration Act was unusual because it loosened restrictions on religious freedom at a time when intolerance was the rule throughout the world. The Reformation had brought on many struggles between Catholics and Protestants, and often religious intolerance spread to the New World.

Rhode Island Colonial Charter

1. Charles II

2. 1663

3. The "hopeful undertakeinge" was the establishment of the Rhode Island Colony.

4. The king showed that he was aware of the colonists' quest for religious freedom when he said that one of the reasons for the charter was to "preserve unto them that libertye, in the true Christian ffaith and worshipp of God, which they have sought with soe much travaill, . . ."

5. According to the charter, this grant of religious freedom would not affect the Church of England because of the great distance of the colony from England.

6. In the following lines, Charles II officially grants religious freedom to the inhabitants of Rhode Island: "our royall will and pleasure is, that noe person within the sayd colonye, at any tyme hereafter, shall bee any wise molested, punished, disquieted, or all in question, for any differences in opinione in matters of religion, . . . but that all and everye person and persons may, from tyme to tyme, and at all tymes hereafter, freelye and fully have and enjoye his and theire owne judgments and consciences, in matters of religious concernments, throughout the tract of lande hereafter mentioned; . . . "

7. Any two of the following may be listed: the colonists had to behave peacefully and quietly, could not use the freedom as an excuse for licentious or profane behavior, or as an excuse for the civil injury or disturbance of others.

8. The king established a civil government for Rhode Island with the following phrase: "they . . . and all such others as now are, or hereafter shall bee admitted and made ffree of the company and societie of our collonie of Providence Plantations, in the Narragansett Bay, in New-England, shall bee, from tyme to tyme, and forever hereafter, a bodie corporate and politique, . . . "

9. Twenty-seven years (the first settlement in Rhode Island was established in 1636).

10. Roger Williams founded Providence, the first settlement in Rhode Island, in 1636. He did so after he was banished from Massachusetts because he demanded greater religious freedom in that colony.

11. The Rhode Island colonial charter was one of the first documents to grant religious freedom in the colonies. Also, Rhode Island was granted more complete freedom than any other colony. Maryland, for example, only granted toleration to Christians. Complete freedom of religion would become an important idea in the Bill of Rights in the U.S. Constitution.

Habeas Corpus Amendment Act

1. Habeas corpus is a writ requiring that a person who has been imprisoned be brought before a judge to determine if he or she is being legally held.

2. a. A gaol is a jail and a gaoler is a jailer.

   b. According to this paragraph, sheriffs and gaolers had delayed in responding to writs of habeas corpus.

   c. This document requires that a sheriff or gaoler respond to a writ of habeas corpus within three days.

   d. Upon the presentation of a writ of habeas corpus, a sheriff or gaoler must take the prisoner indicated in the writ to court before the lord chancellor, the lord keeper of the Great Seal of England, or the judges or barons of the court from which the writ was issued.

   e. When a prisoner is presented to a court on a writ of habeas corpus, the reason why he or she is detained has to be explained.

   f. Treason and felonies are exempted from the requirements of this paragraph.

3. a. If the regular courts are not in session, the prisoner may appeal to the lord chancellor, the lord keeper, or any of the king's justices.

   b. A recognisance is an obligation before a court or a magistrate that binds a person to perform a particular act, such as appear before a court at a designated time.

   c. It means that the prisoner makes a promise when released to appear at the court at a designated time.

4. a. This section applies to treason and felonies.

   b. Oyer and terminer is a British phrase directing the holding of a court to try offenses.

   c. To indict is to officially charge with a crime.

   d. Prisoners who are not indicted and tried by the second court term after they are imprisoned must be released.

5. A prisoner can only be removed from a prison into the custody of an officer of the law through a writ of habeas corpus or some other legal writ.

6. To prevent imprisonment in colonies acquired after the passage of this act, Section XI forbids imprisonment in "any parts, garrisons, islands, or places beyond the seas which are or at any time hereafter shall be within or without the dominions of his Majesty, his heirs or successors . . . "

7. Charles II

8. Australia

9. Article I, Section 9, of the U.S. Constitution says, "The Privilege of the Writ of Habeas Corpus shall not be suspended, unless when in Cases of Rebellion or Invasion the public safety may require it."

10. the Eighth Amendment

11. The privilege of the writ of habeas corpus protects all citizens because it guarantees that people cannot be unreasonably detained without officially being arrested and charged with a crime.

English Bill of Rights

1. William of Orange became king, and his wife Mary became queen.

2. The House of Lords and the House of Commons of the English Parliament wrote this document and presented it to the king and queen.

3. a. To subvert is to undermine in the hopes of destroying. To extirpate is to destroy completely.

   b. The king is accused of trying to subvert and extirpate Protestantism and English laws and liberties.

4. In the third paragraph, the king is accused of dispensing with and suspending laws passed by Parliament.

5. Parliament

6. This paragraph protests the keeping of a standing army in peacetime without the consent of Parliament, and the illegal quartering of soldiers.

7. a. A papist is one who believes in the supremacy of the pope of the Roman Catholic Church.

   b. Papists were allowed to carry arms, and Protestants were not.

8. The four offenses mentioned in this paragraph and the three that follow it are: corrupt and unqualified people serving on juries, excessive bail, excessive fines, and cruel and illegal punishments.

9. The main idea of this paragraph is to state that all of the offenses previously listed are violations of the laws and statutes of England.

10. a. When the king "abdicated the government," he gave up his claim to the throne.

    b. The purpose of the letters written by William of Orange was to direct the English people to elect representatives for Parliament.

11. Answers will vary because of the large number of declarations in the document.

12. This phrase means that the actions of James II against the English people should not serve as precedents for powers a monarch might assume in the future.

13. In this paragraph the new king and queen had to declare that they wholeheartedly opposed the Roman Catholic Church doctrine that excommunicated kings or queens could rightfully be deposed and murdered by their subjects. They also had to declare that no foreign power should have any authority in England.

14. a. This paragraph says that the Parliament and the king and queen will work together to establish laws.

    b. Parliament emphasizes its own powers in this paragraph to prevent William and Mary from denying or subverting Parliament's powers, as James II had done.

    c. Parliament was interested in "preserving a certainty in the succession" to the English throne because without clear-cut rules of succession, confusion and tumult would occur each time an English ruler died.

    d. This paragraph prevents Catholics and people who are married to Catholics from becoming rulers of England.

15. a. *Non obstante* means "notwithstanding" in Latin. Under the principle of *non obstante*, the king could declare that he was exempted from certain laws of Parliament on his own authority.

    b. The only ways in which exceptions to laws passed by Parliament could be made were if dispensations had been granted in the original law or in other laws passed by Parliament.

16. James II was a Roman Catholic.

17. This event was called the Glorious Revolution or the Revolution of 1688.

18. The president has powers similar to those of the English monarch, and Congress has powers similar to those of Parliament.

19. The Eighth Amendment to the U.S. Constitution says "excessive bail shall not be required, nor excessive fines imposed, nor cruel and unusual punishments inflicted."

20. The U.S. government prevents "arbitrary and illegal actions" through the separation of powers into three branches and the checks and balances system.

Pennsylvania Charter of Privileges

1. William Penn

2. Charles II

3. a. The reason given for granting the charter is to insure the further well-being and good government of Pennsylvania.

   b. The privileges of the charter are granted to the "Freemen, Planters, and Adventurers, and other Inhabitants" of Pennsylvania.

   c. The privileges were granted forever.

4. a. Religious freedom is granted in this paragraph.

   b. The qualifications that a person must meet to be eligible for religious freedom are that he or she must "confess and acknowledge *One* almighty God, the Creator, Upholder and Ruler of the World; and profess [himself or herself] obliged to live quietly under the Civil Government . . . "

5. The privilege granted in this paragraph is that all people who profess to believe in Jesus Christ are allowed to serve in government.

6. a. The part of this section that grants the colonists representation in their government is as follows: "there shall be an Assembly yearly chosen, by the Freemen [of Pennsylvania] . . . "

b. Any six of the following may be listed: to choose a speaker and other officers, to judge the qualifications and elections of its own members, to decide when to adjourn, to appoint committees, to prepare bills to be passed into laws, to impeach criminals, to right wrongs, and to have all other customary powers and privileges of an assembly.

7. a. sheriffs and coroners

   b. The freemen of Pennsylvania choose candidates for these offices to present to the governor for nomination.

   c. These officers serve for three years, as long as they behave themselves well.

   d. Vacancies occurring during an officer's term are filled by the governor.

   e. Clerk of the Peace

   f. The justices in the county in which there is a vacancy in the office of Clerk of the Peace select three candidates for the position. The governor then appoints one of the candidates to fill the vacancy.

8. Answers will vary. In general, laws must be written down and kept in a public place so that they cannot be changed without the consent of the people who made them.

9. In Section V, people accused of crimes are granted the same right to call witnesses and receive counsel as their prosecutors have.

10. Section VI grants citizens the privilege of not being forced to go before the governor and council to answer complaints or questions about property.

11. In Section VIII the proprietor of the colony guarantees that the right of religious freedom granted in the first article of the charter would be upheld forever in Pennsylvania.

12. This paragraph guarantees that neither Penn nor his heirs would break the terms of the charter.

13. Pennsylvania means "Penn's woods" or "Penn's forest."

14. Penn was a Quaker. The Quakers had been persecuted in England for their religious beliefs. Penn wanted to make sure that this did not happen in his colony.

15. the U.S. House of Representatives

16. the Sixth Amendment